GOVERNMENT PROCEDURES AND OPERATIONS

GOVERNMENT AWARDS AND OBJECTIONS: BID PROTESTS AND THE GAO

GOVERNMENT PROCEDURES AND OPERATIONS

Additional books in this series can be found on Nova's website under the Series tab.

Additional E-books in this series can be found on Nova's website under the E-book tab.

GOVERNMENT PROCEDURES AND OPERATIONS

GOVERNMENT AWARDS AND OBJECTIONS: BID PROTESTS AND THE GAO

MATTHEW A. SAUTER
EDITOR

Nova Science Publishers, Inc.
New York

For permission to use material from this book please contact us:
Telephone 631-231-7269; Fax 631-231-8175
Web Site: http://www.novapublishers.com

Additional color graphics may be available in the e-book version of this book.

LIBRARY OF CONGRESS CATALOGING-IN-PUBLICATION DATA

Government awards and objections : bid protests and the GAO / editor, Matthew A. Sauter.
p. cm. Includes index.
ISBN 978-1-61728-680-3 (hardcover)
1. Government purchasing--United States. 2. Letting of contracts--United States. 3. Public contracts--United States. 4. United States. Government Accountability Office. I. Sauter, Matthew A. JK1673.G66 2009 352.5'3--dc22

2010038667

Published by Nova Science Publishers, Inc. † New York

CONTENTS

PREFACE

A bid protest is a formal, written objection to an agency's solicitation for bids or offers, cancellation of a solicitation, or award or proposed award of a contract. Bid protests only became part of the federal procurement system in the early 20th century, more than 100 years after the federal government began purchasing goods and services. However, Congress has authorized bid protests in recognition of their role in providing redress to disappointed bidders and offerors and in ensuring the integrity of the federal procurement process. This book provides background on the GAO bid-protest process and examines timeframes, procedures, what issues can be protested, who can file or be a party to a GAO protest and others parameters.

Chapter 1 - Bid protests, especially bid protests filed with the Government Accountability Office (GAO), have recently received increased congressional scrutiny due to protests of high-profile awards and reports that the number of protests is increasing. The potential delay of contract award or performance triggered by a GAO protest, coupled with the increasing number of GAO protests, has also prompted concerns about the impact of protests upon agency operations, especially in the Department of Defense.

Chapter 2 - Bid protests filed with the Government Accountability Office (GAO) have recently received increased congressional scrutiny due to protests of high-profile awards and reports that the number of protests is increasing. The delay of contract award or performance triggered by a GAO protest, coupled with the increasing number of GAO protests, has also prompted concerns about the potential impact of protests upon government agency operations, especially in the Department of Defense.

GAO is one of three forums with authority to hear general bid protests against the government. The GAO's bid-protest process includes some unique features most notably, the automatic stay of contract award or performance during a GAO protest—that make GAO a desirable forum for many disappointed bidders and offerors.

In recent years, the number of protests filed with GAO has steadily increased. Excluding protests from expanded jurisdiction, the number of bid protests increased steadily from approximately 1,150 in Fiscal Year (FY) 2001 to over 1,550 in FY2008, an increase of 37%. However, most of these protests were dismissed, withdrawn by the protester, or settled prior to GAO issuing an opinion. Since FY2001, on average, GAO issued an opinion on only 22% of bid protests; on average, GAO opinions sustained the protest approximately 20% of the time.

Chapters 3 and 4 feature reports to Congress.

Chapter 5 - On July 7, 2004, an old congressional support agency was given a new name, while keeping the same initials (GAO): at that time, the General Accounting Office, established in 1921, was re-designated the Government Accountability Office (P.L. 108-271). The renaming, which came at the request of its head, the Comptroller General (CG) of the United States, was designed to reflect the agency's evolution and additional duties since its creation more than eight decades before.

The Government Accountability Office is the largest of three agencies that provide staff support, research, review, and analysis for Congress. GAO operates under the control and direction of the Comptroller General, who is appointed by the President, with the advice and consent of the Senate, for a 15-year nonrenewable term. A unique arrangement begins the process with a special bicameral commission of legislators from both parties making recommendations to the President. The CG post is currently vacant, with the resignation of David Walker on March 12, 2008.

GAO was established in 1921 as an independent auditor of government agencies and activities by the Budget and Accounting Act. The office was intended to be "independent of the executive departments," the entities it would audit and review. Sometimes called "Congress's watchdog" and its "investigative arm," GAO now provides a variety of services to Congress that extend beyond its original functions and duties, including oversight, investigation, review, and evaluation of executive programs, operations, and activities. Several proposals in the 110th Congress are seen as augmenting GAO's capabilities. These include clarifying its audit authority over the Intelligence Community (H.R. 978 and S. 82) and enhancing its powers to gain access to executive documents (H.R. 6388). In a separate matter, personnel flexibilities powers granted to the Comptroller General in 2004 have generated some controversy in Congress and among GAO employees. As an outgrowth of this and other considerations, GAO staff have set up a new bargaining unit, the first union in the office's history. Legislation has also been proposed that would, among other things, amend GAO's basic authority over personnel and pay matters for employees, provide pay adjustments and reimbursements for certain employees who had not received pay increases in 2006 and 2007, and establish an office of inspector general (H.R. 5683, which has passed the House and Senate and been sent to the President).

In: Government Awards and Objections: Bid... ISBN: 978-1-61728-680-3
Editor: Matthew A. Sauter

Chapter 1

GAO BID PROTESTS: AN OVERVIEW OF TIMEFRAMES AND PROCEDURES*

Kate M. Manuel and Moshe Schwartz

SUMMARY

Bid protests, especially bid protests filed with the Government Accountability Office (GAO), have recently received increased congressional scrutiny due to protests of high-profile awards and reports that the number of protests is increasing. The potential delay of contract award or performance triggered by a GAO protest, coupled with the increasing number of GAO protests, has also prompted concerns about the impact of protests upon agency operations, especially in the Department of Defense.

GAO, the contracting agencies, and the Court of Federal Claims all have authority to hear bid protests; however, GAO hears more protests annually than the Court of Federal Claims, the only other forum for which data are readily available. GAO's bid-protest process includes some unique features most notably, the stay of contract award or performance commonly triggered by a GAO protest—that make GAO a desirable forum for disappointed bidders and offerors.

---

* This is an edited, reformatted and augmented version of a CRS Report for Congress publication dated March 2010.

Legislation and regulations establish what issues may be protested with GAO and who may bring a protest. GAO may hear claims of alleged illegalities or improprieties in solicitations, cancellations of solicitations, or awards or proposed awards of contracts. It is, however, barred from hearing certain issues, such as challenges to small business size certifications. Any "interested party"—or actual or prospective bidder or offeror whose direct economic interest would be affected by the award of the contract or by failure to award it—may file a protest.

Procedures for bringing and conducting GAO protests are designed to ensure "the inexpensive and expeditious resolution of [bid] protests." Protesters need not file formal briefs or technical pleadings, can represent themselves, and can have protests decided without hearings. All protests are to be resolved within 100 calendar days of their filing, and deadlines for mandatory and optional events within the GAO bid-protest process ensure decisions can be reached within this timeframe.

Filing a GAO protest generally triggers an automatic stay of contract award or performance during the pendency of the protest. A similar stay does not result when protests are filed with the Court of Federal Claims. Agencies can, however, override stays because urgent and compelling circumstances will not permit waiting for GAO's decision, or because performance of the contract is in the best interests of the United States. Agencies must inform GAO of their override decisions, but GAO cannot prevent an agency override.

GAO may deny or sustain a protest. A denial allows the agency to proceed with the challenged award. When GAO sustains a protest, it also makes recommendations to the agency about the challenged award, such as re-competing the contract or issuing a new solicitation. GAO's recommendations are not legally binding upon the agency because the "separation of powers" doctrine precludes legislative branch agencies, such as GAO, from controlling the actions of executive branch agencies. However, the agency is to notify GAO if it does not fully implement GAO's recommendations. GAO is, then, to inform Congress of agency noncompliance. Agencies comply with GAO recommendations in most protests. However, compliance with GAO recommendations, or reliance on GAO precedent, does not immunize agencies from court challenges to their procurement actions.

Protesters disappointed with GAO's decision can seek reconsideration from GAO. They can also "appeal" GAO's decision by filing a bid protest with the Court of Federal Claims.

INTRODUCTION

Protests of high-profile awards and reports that the number of protests is increasing have recently prompted congressional and public interest in bid protests, particularly bid protests filed with the Government Accountability Office (GAO). The number of protests filed with GAO increased by 17% between FY2007 and FY2008 and by 20% between FY2008 and FY2009, in part because of GAO's recently expanded jurisdiction over task and delivery order, A-76, and Transportation Security Administration protests.[1] Some of these protests involved high-profile procurements, such as the Air Force's aerial refueling tanker and combat, search, and rescue (CSAR-X) helicopter,[2] and prompted congressional hearings or proposed legislation.[3] The Department of Defense (DOD) has also expressed concerns about the effects that the delay of contract award or performance frequently triggered by a GAO protest have upon DOD operations.[4] Partly in response to DOD's concerns, the House Armed Services Committee of the 110th Congress requested, when authorizing DOD's budget for FY2009, that GAO investigate and report on the impact of bid protests on DOD.[5] GAO issued its report on April 9, 2009, finding that its existing authorities were sufficient to deal with allegedly frivolous protests and that further attempts to discourage such protests could "have the unintended consequences of discouraging participation in federal contracting and, in turn, limiting competition."[6] However, despite GAO's report, concerns about "frivolous" GAO protests have recently been increasing, particularly among contractors.[7]

This chapter is one of two providing Congress with background on the GAO bid-protest process. It provides an overview of the timeframes and procedures in a GAO bid protest, including (1) what issues can be protested with GAO; (2) who can file or be a party to a GAO protest; (3) the procedures for bringing and resolving GAO protests; (4) the timeframes involved in GAO protests; (5) the automatic stay of contract award or performance triggered by a GAO protest, as well as the basis for agency overrides of automatic stays and judicial review of agency override determinations; (6) the basis and effects of GAO decisions; and (7) reconsideration and "appeal" of GAO decisions. Its companion report is CRS Report R40227, *GAO Bid Protests: Trends, Analysis, and Options for Congress*, by Moshe Schwartz and Kate M. Manuel, which analyzes recent trends in bid protests filed with GAO, particularly protests involving DOD.[8]

Background

A bid protest is a formal, written objection to an agency's solicitation for bids or offers, cancelation of a solicitation, or award or proposed award of a contract.[9] Bid protests only became part of the federal procurement system in the early 20th century, more than 100 years after the federal government began purchasing goods and services. However, Congress has authorized bid protests in recognition of their role in providing redress to disappointed bidders and offerors and in ensuring the integrity of the federal procurement process. Congress has thus authorized three administrative and judicial forums to hear bid protests against the federal government.

Historical Development of Federal Bid-Protest Mechanisms

GAO first began hearing bid protests in the early 20th century on the theory that its authority to settle and adjust "all claims and demands" against the United States encompassed bid protests.[10] The federal courts did not then hear protests, although at least some agencies did. In fact, after GAO first began hearing bid protests, the federal courts held that they lacked jurisdiction to hear them. In *Perkins v. Lukens Steel Company*, the Supreme Court said that federal courts could not hear bid protests because the existing procurement laws did not confer standing on actual or potential bidders or offerors who had been disappointed in their dealings with the federal government.[11] The Court said that these procurement laws were strictly for the government's benefit, "for the purpose of keeping its own house in order."[12]

Several decades later, the federal courts came to hold that the Administrative Procedure Act (APA) authorized them to hear bid protests,[13] and Congress later explicitly granted bid protest jurisdiction to GAO with the Competition in Contracting Act (CICA) of 1984.[14] However, GAO's long history of handling bid protests, coupled with several unique aspects of the GAO bid-protest process, most notably the stay of contract award or performance that generally results from the filing of a GAO protest, make it the primary locus for federal bid protests.

Purposes of Bid-Protest Processes

Although disappointed bidders or offerors would generally have no right to protest if Congress did not provide for this right, Congress has chosen to authorize several administrative or judicial forums to hear bid protests for several reasons. First, protest mechanisms ensure that entities doing business with the government can air their complaints about governmental contracting processes and obtain relief. Without such mechanisms, certain frustrations that citizens have with their government could remain unaddressed. Additionally, absent such mechanisms, entities might be less willing to do business with the government, which could diminish competition for government contracts and drive up prices. Second, protest mechanisms enhance the accountability of procurement officials and government agencies by highlighting and correcting mistakes and misconduct. This accountability helps to ensure the integrity of the procurement system. If the government's procurement system were perceived as corrupt or ineffective, contractors might be less willing to compete for government contracts, and the price at which the government acquires goods and services could increase. A corrupt or ineffective procurement system could also waste taxpayers' money.

These benefits of bid protests are not costless, however; protests can impede the prompt and efficient acquisition of goods and services needed by the government. Particularly when award or performance of a contested contract is stayed by the filing of a bid protest, as happens with many GAO protests, protests can delay agency procurement actions. Protests also require agency officials to spend time in explaining their conduct to disappointed bidders and offerors and in defending their conduct before administrative or judicial forums. Moreover, fear of possible protests may increase the time and energy that agencies expend in documenting their procurement decisions. Congress has, however, historically viewed the benefits of bid protests as outweighing these costs.

THE GAO BID PROTEST PROCESS

CICA charges GAO with "provid[ing] for the inexpensive and expeditious resolution of [bid] protests" to "the maximum extent practicable."[15] GAO has attempted to meet these goals through the use of timeframes and procedures partly prescribed by statute and partly established by administrative rule making.[16]

What Issues Can be Protested with GAO?

Under CICA, disappointed bidders or offerors can protest[17] to GAO about alleged illegalities or improprieties in (1) solicitations or other requests by federal agencies for offers for contracts for goods or services, (2) cancellations of solicitations or other requests for offers by federal agencies, (3) awards or proposed awards of contracts by federal agencies, or (4) terminations or cancellations of contract awards by federal agencies *if* the protest alleges that the termination or cancellation was based on improprieties in the contract's award.[18] The alleged and protested illegality or impropriety can exist prior to the contract award, as when a contractor claims that some aspect of the solicitation would improperly disadvantage it in competing for the contract. Alternately, the alleged and protested illegality or impropriety can arise with the contract, as when a contractor claims that the government failed to follow the rules for the competition or otherwise acted improperly in awarding the contract to the protestor's competitor. Starting in FY2008, under additional jurisdiction granted to GAO by Congress, protested illegalities or improprieties could include matters relating to agencies' issuance of task orders, contracting out under Office of Management and Budget (OMB) Circular A-76, and Transportation Security Administration contracts.[19]

GAO regulations, however, exclude certain issues from GAO protests even when these issues are integrally linked to the formation of a government contract. These issues include the following:

- challenges to small business size standards and standard industrial classifications; issuance of or refusal to issue certificates of competency under Section 8(b)(7) of the Small Business Act; and determinations to procure particular requirements through the Minority Small Business and Capital Ownership Development Program (commonly known as the 8(a) Program);[20]
- alleged procurement integrity violations which the protester did not to report to the agency responsible for the alleged violations within 14 days of discovering them;[21]
- procurements by agencies other than federal agencies as defined in Section 3 of the Federal Property and Administrative Services Act;[22]
- awards or proposed awards of subcontracts, unless the agency awarding the prime contract had requested in writing that subcontract protests be handled by GAO as non-statutory protests;[23]
- suspensions or debarments of contractors by agencies;[24] or

- decisions by agency tender officials to file or not file protests in connection with public-private competitions.[25]

Who Can File or Be a Party to a GAO Protest?

By statute, a GAO bid protest may be filed by any "interested party,"[26] or any "actual or prospective bidder or offeror whose direct economic interest would be affected by the award of the contract or by failure to award the contract."[27] This focus upon direct economic interest in determining who is an interested party means that a larger number of contractors can bring pre-award protests than can bring post-award protests. Prior to the award, contractors who are considering bidding or offering generally qualify as interested parties. After an award, however, only contractors who bid on the contract or submitted offers qualify as interested parties because only they were eligible for the award.[28] Moreover, because of the focus on *direct* economic interest, GAO often requires that contractors both (1) have bid or offered and (2) be next in line for the award if the protest is sustained for them to be recognized as interested parties.[29] Because they lack these direct economic interests, non-contractors—such as concerned citizens—are not interested parties who can bring GAO bid protests.

In addition to prospective or actual bidders or offerors, other parties to GAO bid protests include the agency conducting the challenged procurement and, potentially, one or more intervenors. Intervenors enter protests to protect their status as awardees or potential awardees under the protested procurement. When the contract has not yet been awarded, GAO permits all bidders or offerors who "appear to have a substantial prospect of receiving an award if the protest is denied" to intervene.[30] Similarly, when the contract has been awarded, GAO permits the winning bidder or offeror to intervene.[31]

Procedures for Bringing and Resolving GAO Protests: "Inexpensive Resolution"

"No formal briefs or other technical forms of pleading or motion are required" for an interested party to file a GAO bid protest.[32] For GAO to consider its protest, a protestor need only (1) identify the contracting agency and the solicitation or contract number; (2) set forth a detailed statement of the legal and factual grounds of protest, including copies of relevant documents;

(3) establish that the protester is an interested party making a timely protest; and (4) state the relief requested (e.g., termination or re-competition of a contract).[33] In their filings, protesters may also request protective orders, specific documents from the agency, or a hearing before GAO.[34]

GAO allows contractors to represent themselves in bid protest proceedings and to have their protests resolved based on paper filings without a hearing. Although they may use the services of an attorney in preparing or prosecuting a GAO protest, protesters are not required to do so[35] and can avoid the costs of attorneys' fees by representing themselves. Similarly, resolution of the protest based upon documents filed by the protester and the agency, as opposed to by hearing, allows protesters to avoid the costs of traveling to Washington, D.C., where GAO is located, for hearings.[36] Hearings are relatively rare in GAO protests. Between FY2005 and FY2009, only 6%-12% of GAO cases annually entailed hearings.[37] Moreover, when held, hearings are less formal than hearings in federal court, with the parties and GAO determining at a pre-hearing conference what procedures will be followed, what issues will be considered, and what witnesses will testify.[38]

All these factors, as well as the strict timeframes for resolving GAO protests, described below, can make GAO a less expensive venue in which to conduct bid protests than the Court of Federal Claims. Protesters in the Court of Federal Claims are, in contrast, generally more likely to be represented by attorneys and have hearings on their protests.[39] Their protests can also take longer to resolve.[40] However, some commentators have wondered (1) whether GAO's comparatively quicker and less formal procedures make GAO more likely than the Court of Federal Claims to issue erroneous decisions and (2) whether GAO is the best forum for "awards involving complex systems or services with values rising to the hundreds of millions of dollars or more."[41]

Timeframes Involved in GAO Protests: "Expeditious Resolution"

GAO is to adhere to strict timeframes—resolving protests within 100 calendar days of their filing—to ensure that protesters receive prompt resolution of their claims and to prevent bid protests from delaying the procurement of necessary goods and services by government agencies.[42] A protester who files a bid protest with the Court of Federal Claims could, in contrast, potentially wait over 100 days before the court hears its case[43] and would not have the award or performance of the contract stayed for the duration of the protest, as generally happens with GAO protests. This section outlines the timeframes for the main steps in GAO bid protests.

Initial Filings by Interested Parties

The timeframes within which interested parties must, by regulation, file bid protests with GAO depend upon the circumstances prompting the protest. Alleged improprieties in solicitations that are apparent prior to bid opening or the time set for receipt of initial proposals must be protested before the bid opening or the time set for receipt of initial proposals.[44] Other alleged improprieties must be protested no later than 10 calendar days after they become known, or should have become known, whichever is earlier, unless the protest challenges "a procurement conducted on the basis of competitive proposals under which a debriefing is requested and, when requested, is required."[45] Protests filed after these deadlines are untimely, and GAO generally dismisses them.[46] GAO considers untimely protests only when the protester shows good cause for its late filing or when GAO determines that the protest raises "issues significant to the procurement system."[47] Would-be protesters that miss GAO filing deadlines can still file bid protests with the Court of Federal Claims within six years of the events prompting the protest, however.[48]

GAO Notice to the Agency

Once a protest is filed with GAO, it must notify the federal agency whose contracting activities are being protested within one working day of receiving the protest.[49] This notice is important for two reasons. First, the agency's receipt of GAO's notice generally marks the beginning of an automatic stay of the award or performance of the contract. Under CICA, if a protest is filed within 10 days of the contract award or within 5 days of a debriefing, a federal agency that has been notified of a GAO bid protest may not award or authorize performance of the contested contract until GAO decides the protest.[50] Second, the agency's receipt of GAO's notice marks the beginning of the 30-calendar-day period within which the agency must generally respond to the GAO protest.[51]

Agency's Response and Protester's Reply

When responding to a GAO bid protest, the agency must file a report with GAO, generally within 30 calendar days of receiving notice of the protest.[52] Under GAO regulations, this chapter must include

> ... the contracting officer's statement of the relevant facts, including a best estimate of the contract value, a memorandum of law, and a list and a copy of all relevant documents, or portions of documents, not previously produced, including, as appropriate: the protest; the bid or proposals submitted by the protester; the bid or proposal of the firm which is being considered for the award, or whose bid or proposal is being protested; all evaluation documents; the solicitation, including the specifications; the abstract of bids or offers; and any other relevant documents.[53]

Table 1. Timeframes of Important Events in the GAO Bid-Protest Process For Protests Other than Those Based on Improprieties in Solicitations That Were Apparent Prior to the Bid Opening or the Time Set for Receipt of Initial Proposals

Event	Normal Timeframes	Express Timeframes
Filing of protest with GAO	No more than 10 calendar days after the protested conduct	No more than 10 calendar days after the protested conduct
Notice of the protest sent from GAO to the agency	Within 1 working day of the protest's being filed	Within 1 working day of the protest's being filed
Agency's report on the protested procurement sent to GAO	Within 30 calendar days of the agency's receiving notice of the protest	Within 20 calendar days of the agency's receiving notice of the protest
Protester's reply to the agency's report	Within 10 calendar days of the filing of the agency report	Within 5 calendar days of the filing of the agency report
GAO's decision on the protest	Within 100 calendar days of the protest's being filed	Within 65 calendar days of the protest's being filed

Source: Congressional Research Service

The agency can avoid filing this chapter only when it, or an intervenor, requests and is granted dismissal of the protest by GAO before the report is due.[54]

After the agency's report is filed, the protester then has 10 calendar days to submit written comments on the agency's report to GAO.[55] If the protester fails to submit such comments, GAO is required, by its own regulations, to dismiss the protest.[56]

Issuance of GAO's Decision on a Protest

GAO generally must issue its final decision on a bid protest within 100 calendar days of the protest's filing.[57] This timeframe can be shortened to 65 calendar days if the Comptroller General determines, either at the request of a party or upon his or her own initiative, that the protest should be treated under the "express option," which allows for faster-than-usual decisions.[58] GAO can also dismiss a protest that is frivolous, or that does not state, on its face, a valid basis for protest, at any time,[59] even before the agency files its report with GAO.[60] GAO can similarly issue a summary decision on a protest at any time.[61]

The importance that Congress attaches to the expeditious resolution of protests by GAO is indicated by the fact that GAO would have to report to Congress on any instance in which GAO fails to issue its final decision on a protest within 100 calendar days of the protest's filing. According to GAO, GAO has never had to make such a report to Congress.

Timeframes for Other Optional Events in the GAO Bid-Protest Process

Similarly short timeframes apply to other optional events in the GAO bid protest process:

- protesters must request expedited review under GAO's "express option" within five calendar days of filing the protest;[62]
- protesters who want GAO to hold hearings on the protest must request a hearing "as early as possible in the protest process";[63]
- protesters must request any additional documents whose existence or relevance becomes evident only after the filing of the agency report within two calendar days of discovering their existence;[64] and
- parties must file written comments on any hearing within five calendar days of the hearing.[65]

Automatic Stays of Contract Award or Performance during GAO Protests

Under CICA, the filing of a bid protest with GAO generally triggers an automatic stay, or postponement, of contract award or performance. With pre-award bid protests, an agency may not award the contested contract until the protest has been resolved.[66] Similarly, with post-award bid protests, the agency must withhold authorization of performance under the contract while the protest is pending.[67] If authorization has not been withheld, the agency must "immediately direct the contractor to cease performance under the contract" until the protest is resolved.[68]

These bid-protest stays, sometimes called "CICA stays," are a key aspect of the GAO bid-protest process,[69] which Congress intended to strengthen.[70] Congress did not provide for similar stays when bid protests are filed with the Court of Federal Claims. Rather, bid protesters filing suit in the Court of Federal Claims must meet the court's customary requirements for temporary restraining orders or preliminary injunctions in order to effect a delay of the agency's procurement activities similar to that generally occurring automatically when a GAO protest is filed.[71] This difference between bid protests at GAO and those at the Court of Federal Claims has prompted some commentators to worry that the stays triggered by GAO protests encourage contractors to "game the system." Such commentators worry that contractors knowingly file meritless protests with GAO in order to harass their competitors and delay awards to them, or in the hopes of obtaining short-term contracts from the government during the pendency of the GAO protest.[72] These commentators also worry that the public interest, as embodied in the contract to be awarded or performed, is neglected during the stay.[73]

Agency Override of Bid-Protest Stays

Even if it takes the maximum time, a GAO bid protest does not necessarily delay contract award or performance for up to 100 calendar days. This is in part because CICA also provides grounds for agency overrides of automatic bid-protest stays.[74] Agencies may override bid-protest stays upon two grounds: (1) "urgent and compelling circumstances which significantly affect interests of the United States will not permit waiting for the decision of the Comptroller General,"[75] or (2) "performance of the contract is in the best interests of the United States."[76] Only "urgent and compelling circumstances" may be asserted when GAO bid protests are filed prior to the award of the contract.[77] Either "urgent and compelling circumstances" or the "best interests of the United States" may be asserted when GAO bid protests are filed after the award of the contract.[78]

Beyond when the grounds may be asserted, few other differences are apparent between the circumstances in which agencies can invoke "urgent and compelling circumstances" and those in which they can invoke the "best interests of the United States," as **Table 2** illustrates.[79] Some courts and commentators have suggested, however, that an agency's invocation of "urgent and compelling circumstances" has more serious overtones and ought to receive more deference than an agency's invocation of the "best interests of the United States."[80]

Table 2. Examples of Procurements Involving "Urgent and Compelling Circumstances" or the "Best Interests of the United States"

Urgent and Compelling Circumstances	Best Interests of the United States
• Canine services for Army Special Forces in Afghanistan: agency record showed adverse consequences, in the form of security breaches at military installations, without the override; the override was only for a bridge contract, with the agency planning a new solicitation within a year; and the only alleged harm to the protester was the dissatisfaction of its employees.[a]	• Cockpit video recording systems recorders for F/A-18 aircraft: agency record showed that the agency conducted a proper evaluation in making the initial award; the override involved a 1 year contract; failure to override would interfere with the aircraft's deployment to Bosnia and troop training; and the public interest required that the troops be well equipped.[d]
• Maintenance & refuse services at Navy housing facility: agency record showed that services under the contract were essential to the health, safety, and morale of military personnel; the protester's allegations of harm were speculative; and the public interest would be harmed if the protester, which was not a small business, got an award set aside for a small business.[b]	• Training services for a "top gun" school: protester alleged only speculative harm, claiming it would never "get on base again" if it lost the protest; the agency record showed that the contract was key to the success of a weapons school whose operations had already been interrupted; and protecting national security by ensuring adequate training was in the public interest.[e]
• Maintenance & support services for Border Patrol academy: agency record showed that the protester, who was the incumbent contractor, had performed inadequately and could not continue to perform during the protest; and time pressures required the award of a new contract.[c]	• Spectrum management engineering services: agency record showed that performance under the protested contract was time-critical and that the winning offeror was only source with personnel qualified to perform the work.[f]

Source: Congressional Research Service

Notes: All examples are taken from federal court cases in which the courts found that the agency had acted reasonably in overriding a CICA stay upon the grounds of "urgent and compelling circumstances" or the "best interests of the United States."

a. EOD Tech., Inc. v. United States, 82 Fed. Cl. 12 (2008).

b. Superior Services, Inc. v. Dalton, 851 F. Supp. 381 (S.D. Cal. 1994).

c. Ramcor Servs. Group, Inc. v. United States, 185 F.3d 1286 (Fed. Cir. 1999).

d. Teac Am., Inc. v. U.S. Dep't of the Navy, 876 F. Suppl. 289 (D.D.C. 1995).

e. SDS Int'l Inc. v. United States, 55 Fed. Cl. 363 (2003).

f. Alion Science & Tech. Corp. v. United States, 69 Fed. Cl. 14 (2005).

Any agency override, upon any basis, requires a written finding that grounds for the override exist, and the Comptroller General must be notified of this finding.[81]

GAO and Agency Override Determinations

Although agencies are required by law to inform GAO of their override determinations, GAO does not review the agency's override determination and cannot reverse it. GAO lacks authority and jurisdiction to keep the agency from proceeding to award or authorize performance of the contract under the override. All GAO can do is report on agency overrides to Congress, as it did in its annual reports until FY2002.[82] Potential congressional awareness of agency override determinations may act as a brake on agency overrides.

Judicial Review of Agency Override Determinations

Outside of the agency itself, the only entity that can reverse an agency override determination and reinstate the delay of contract award or performance that a GAO bid protest triggers is a federal court—currently the Court of Federal Claims[83]—acting on the petition of the protester. To achieve such an outcome, the court would have to grant the protester's motion to restrain or enjoin the government from awarding the contract or authorizing performance under it.[84]

Although courts once exempted agency determinations as to the "best interests of the United States" from judicial review[85] and gave substantial deference to agency determinations as to "best interests" and "urgent and compelling circumstances,"[86] the Court of Federal Claims has not infrequently enjoined agency overrides after subjecting the agency's override determination to "searching inquiry."[87] Override determinations based on considerations of national security or national defense sometimes receive greater deference from the Court of Federal Claims,[88] but not even these considerations guarantee victory for agencies.[89]

Basis and Effects of GAO Decisions

GAO is charged by statute with "deciding" all bid protests filed in accordance with GAO regulations.[90] When deciding a protest, GAO is not to substitute its judgment for the agency's, or conduct *de novo* review of agency procurement activities and processes.[91] Rather, GAO is to consider only whether the agency complied with procurement statutes or regulations, as well as had reasonable bases and adequate documentation, in its decision making.[92]

Denials, Sustainments, and GAO Recommendations

When GAO finds no illegalities or other problems, it is to deny the protest, leaving the agency free to award the contract, or authorize performance under it, barring a court order to the contrary. When GAO finds illegalities or other problems, however, it would sustain the protest and may recommend that the agency (1) refrain from exercising its options under the contract, (2) re-compete the contract, (3) issue a new solicitation, (4) terminate the contract, (5) award the contract consistent with the requirements of statutes or regulations, or (6) implement any other recommendation that the "Comptroller General determines to be necessary in order to promote compliance with procurement statutes and regulations."[93] In deciding which of these options to recommend, GAO considers all the circumstances surrounding the procurement or proposed procurement.[94] This includes the seriousness of the agency's procurement deficiency, the degree of prejudice to the other parties and the integrity of the procurement system, the extent of performance, the cost to the government, the urgency of the procurement, and the potential impact of any GAO recommendation upon the agency's mission.[95] Because GAO is a legislative branch agency, it could not constitutionally "compel" executive branch agencies to "obey" its recommendations because of the separation of powers doctrine.[96]

Along with its recommendations sustaining the protest, GAO can also recommend that the agency conducting the procurement pay to the protester the costs of filing and pursuing the protest, including reasonable attorneys' fees; the fees for consultants and expert witnesses; and the expenses of preparing the bid or protest.[97] When GAO recommends that an agency pay costs, the agency must either pay the costs promptly or report to the Comptroller General its reasons for not paying.[98] The agency must also attempt to reach an agreement with the protester on the costs to be paid.[99] If agreement cannot be reached, the protester can request that GAO recommend to the agency an amount to be paid.[100]

Legal Effect of GAO Recommendations

Even when GAO finds that the agency engaged in illegal or improper conduct and sustains the protest, however, the agency is not legally required to implement the recommendations in GAO's decision. GAO recommendations lack the force of law and are not binding upon the parties. In fact, a decision by GAO on a protest does not preclude a protester from later filing suit on the same matter in the Court of Federal Claims.[101]

Agencies typically fully adopt GAO recommendations, nonetheless, as **Table 3** illustrates. According to GAO's annual reports to Congress, in only four cases between FY2001 and FY2009 did an agency decline to fully adopt GAO's recommendations. However, GAO reports are based on statutory requirements focused upon a procuring agency's implementation of specific recommendations regarding a particular solicitation, proposed award, or award within a relatively short time frame (65 days):

> If the Federal agency fails to implement fully the recommendations of the Comptroller General under this subsection with respect to a solicitation for a contract or an award or proposed award of a contract within 60 days after receiving the recommendations, the head of the procuring activity responsible for that contract shall report such failure to the Comptroller General not later than 5 days after the end of such 60-day period.[102]

Table 3. Number of Cases in Which Agencies Did Not Fully Adopt GAO Recommendations Per Fiscal Year 2001-2009

Fiscal Year	Number of Cases
2001	0
2002	1[a]
2003	2[b]
2004	0
2005	0
2006	0
2007	0
2008	0
2009	1[c]

Source: Congressional Research Service using data from GAO

a. Rockwell Elec. Commerce Corp., B-286201.6, .8 (Comp. Gen. Aug. 30, 2001 and Mar. 5, 2002).

b. Consolidated Eng'g Servs., Inc., B-291345, .2 (Comp. Gen. Dec. 23, 2002); Symplicity Corp., B-291902, Apr. 29, 2003.

c. Mission Critical Solutions, B-401057 (Comp. Gen. Dec. May 4, 2009).

The reports thus do not necessarily capture decisions whose underlying logic the executive branch disagrees with at a later date. GAO issued such a decision, which is not addressed in either its FY2008 or FY2009 reports to Congress, on September 19, 2008, in *International Program Group, Inc.*[103] This decision was the first of two—the second of which was issued on May 4, 2009[104]—in which GAO construed the Small Business Act to require that set-asides for Historically Underutilized Business Zone (HUBZone) small businesses take "precedence" over set-asides for other categories of small businesses.[105] It was only after the second decision that the Obama Administration indicated that it would not accord HUBZone set-asides precedence over set-asides for service-disabled veteran-owned and 8(a) small businesses because it disagrees with GAO's construction of the Small Business Act.[106] However, the Obama Administration's discretion regarding whether to comply with GAO's recommendations on HUBZone and 8(a) set-asides was effectively removed on March 2, 2010, when the Court of Federal Claims held that HUBZone set-asides have precedence over 8(a) set-asides.[107] If this decision is not reversed on appeal and Congress does not enact proposed legislation that would amend the HUBZone Act (H.R. 3729, S. 1489), agencies must use HUBZone set-asides instead of 8(a) set-asides whenever possible.

The high degree of agency deference to GAO recommendations arguably reflects the scrutiny that Congress gives to agency decisions not to fully implement GAO recommendations. By statute, agencies have 60 calendar days within which to fully adopt GAO recommendations. Any agency that does not do so must promptly notify GAO, which then promptly notifies four congressional committees.[108] Once aware that an agency is not fully adopting GAO's recommendations,

Congress can exercise oversight or take legislative action compelling agency compliance, if it so chooses.[109]

Compliance with GAO Precedent or Recommendations as a Violation of the Administrative Procedure Act

Compliance with GAO precedent or recommendations does not necessarily immunize the agency from all future legal challenges to its actions or liability. Two recent Court of Federal Claims decisions illustrate how an agency could be found to have acted arbitrarily, capriciously, and in abuse of discretion, in violation of the Administrative Procedure Act (APA), by following GAO precedents or adopting GAO recommendations.

In the first case, *Geo-Seis Helicopters, Inc. v. United States*, the Military Sealift Command (MSC) accepted amendments to the winning bid after the bid closing date in reliance on GAO precedent allowing agencies to issue amendments that extend the closing date after the closing date has passed—but arguably contrary to the "late is late" rule of Federal Acquisition Regulation Section 52.215-1(c)(3)(ii)(A).[110] A losing bidder protested the MSC's actions to GAO and then filed suit in the Court of Federal Claims after GAO denied the protest.[111] The Court of Federal Claims found that the MSC violated the APA by relying on GAO precedent: "The refusal of the [MSC's] Contracting Officer to adhere to the categorical reality of the 'late is late' rule renders arbitrary her decision to accept [the winning bidder's] first and second revised proposals."[112]

In the second case, *Grunley Walsh International, LLC v. United States*, as a result of GAO recommendations, the State Department adopted GAO's interpretation of a statutory business-volume requirement for bidders on embassy construction contracts in place of its own previous interpretation.[113] Under GAO's interpretation, a bidder that had pre-qualified under the State Department's interpretation had its pre-qualification withdrawn.[114] This bidder filed suit against the State Department in the Court of Federal Claims alleging that the State Department's actions violated the APA even if they comported with GAO's recommendations.[115] The Court of Federal Claims found for the bidder, noting that the GAO recommendation "was ... irrational because it misread both the actual language of the statute and the legislative history" and the State Department acted irrationally in adopting it.[116]

Although the Court of Federal Claims and other courts had reversed GAO decisions in other cases,[117] as discussed below, prior courts did not so explicitly link following GAO's recommendations with violations of the APA.[118] *Geo-Seis Helicopters* and *Grunley Walsh* thus highlight more clearly than previous cases agencies' dilemmas in complying with CICA. Failure to fully implement GAO recommendations triggers reporting to Congress and possible congressional oversight, while complying with GAO recommendations could leave agencies vulnerable to charges of having violated the APA.

Reconsideration and "Appeal" of GAO Decisions

Much like agencies can decline to fully implement GAO recommendations that they are dissatisfied with, protesters who are dissatisfied with GAO decisions can also potentially avoid them by (1) requesting reconsideration from GAO or (2) "appealing" to the Court of Federal Claims. Disappointed agencies and intervenors can also request reconsideration from GAO, but need not "appeal" to the Court of Federal Claims because the agency can always decline to follow GAO recommendations.

Reconsideration of GAO Decisions

Any party to a GAO protest can request reconsideration of GAO's decision from GAO.[119] Such a request must be made within 10 calendar days after the basis for reconsideration is known or should be known, whichever is earlier.[120] GAO does not consider requests for reconsideration that lack detailed statements of the factual or legal grounds upon which reversal or modification is sought, "specifying any errors of law made or information not previously considered."[121] GAO will also summarily dismiss any reconsideration requests that fail to state valid bases for reconsideration or are untimely.[122] Filing a request for reconsideration with GAO does not stay award or performance of a disputed contract like filing a bid protest with GAO does.[123]

As **Table 4** illustrates, GAO receives far fewer requests for reconsideration than bid protests each year, and GAO seldom changes its recommendations upon reconsideration.[124]

Table 4. Comparative Number of Requests for Reconsideration and Protests Received and Closed by GAO Per Fiscal Year 2001-2009

Fiscal Year	Protests		Reconsideration Requests	
	Received	Closed	Received	Closed
2001	1084	1040	62	58
2002	1139	1072	65	61
2003	1269	1181	83	63
2004	1387	1334	98	71
2005	1285	1285	71	56
2006	1270	1224	57	50
2007	1318	1300	93	93
2008	1563	1506	89	71
2009	1898	1822	91	96

Source: Congressional Research Service using data from GAO

"Appeal" of GAO Decisions

In addition to requesting reconsideration from GAO, disappointed protesters can effectively "appeal" GAO's decisions to the Court of Federal Claims by filing suit alleging that the agency's procurement activities were "arbitrary, capricious, an abuse of discretion, or otherwise not in accordance with the law" in violation of the Administrative Procedure Act (APA).[125] The focus of the suit in the Court of Federal Claims is the agency's procurement activities, not GAO's decision *per se*. However, GAO's decision makes up part of the agency record that is reviewed by the Court of Federal Claims,[126] and the Court of Federal Claims gives some deference to GAO decisions on questions of fact.[127]

Table 5. Comparison of the Total Number of Bid Protests and the Number of Bid Protests "Appealing" GAO Decisions Resulting in Published Opinions of the Court of Federal Claims Per Calendar Year 2001-2007

Year	Total Bid-Protest Decisions	Bid-Protest Decisions with Prior GAO Decisions
2001	33 total (31 unique)[a]	12 total (11 unique)
2002	19 total (17 unique)	6 total (6 unique)
2003	33 total (31 unique)	17 total (17 unique)
2004	49 total (41 unique)	20 total (19 unique)
2005	46 total (40 unique)	23 total (22 unique)
2006	46 total (40 unique)	25 total (24 unique)
2007	50 total (42 unique)	23 total (19 unique)

Source: Congressional Research Service

Notes: Not all Court of Federal Claims cases result in a published opinions. The Court of Federal Claims is estimated to issue one published opinion for every five matters disposed of. Steven L. Schooner, The Future: Scrutinizing the Empirical Case for the Court of Federal Claims, 71 *Geo. Wash. L. Rev.* 714, 751(2003).

a. Some bid protests result in multiple published decisions from the court when, for example, the court decides on motions for temporary restraining orders or injunctions; requests for dismissal; requests for summary judgment; the merits of the case; and motions for attorneys fees, or sanctions for filing frivolous lawsuits.

In reviewing the agency's action, the court does not substitute its judgment for that of the agency.[128] Rather, it looks at the agency's record of the procurement to determine whether the procurement official's decision lacked a rational basis, or the procurement procedure involved a violation of law or procedure.[129] In determining whether the procurement official's decision had a rational basis, the court considers whether (1) the agency relied on factors Congress did not intend it to consider in making its decision; (2) failed to consider an important aspect of the problem; or (3) offered an explanation for its action contrary to the evidence before it, or so implausible it could not be ascribed to a difference of opinion or the product of agency expertise.[130]

As **Table 5** illustrates, comparatively few of the hundreds of bid protests that GAO hears per year are "appealed" to the Court of Federal Claims. Many of the bid protests that the Court of Federal Claims hears are, according to CRS research, filed directly with it without prior GAO protests.

A Court of Federal Claims protest, even one "appealing" a prior GAO decision, does not trigger an automatic stay of the agency's award of the contract or authorization of performance under it.

Rather, a bid protester in the Court of Federal Claims must file and prevail upon a motion for a temporary restraining order or preliminary injunction to effect a delay of the agency's procurement actions similar to that generally occurring automatically when a GAO protest is filed.

End Notes

[1] GAO, *GAO Bid Protest Annual Report to the Congress for Fiscal Year 2009*, Jan. 8, 2010, *available at* http://www.gao.gov/special.pubs/bidpro09.pdf (noting that GAO handled 1,989 cases in FY2009). This includes 91 requests for reconsideration and 168 protests filed as a result of GAO's expanded jurisdiction.

[2] *See, e.g.*, Dana Hedgepeth & Robert O'Harrow, Jr., Air Force Faulted over Handling of Tanker Deal, *Washington Post*, June 19, 2008, at A1; Michael Fabey, Lockheed Martin Files Another CSAR-X Protest, *Aviation Week*, June 12, 2007, *available at* http://www.aviationweek.com/aw/generic/story.jsp?id=news/CSAR061207.xml&headline=Lockheed%20Martin%20Files%20Another%20CSAR-X%20Protest&channel=defense.

[3] *See, e.g.*, Air Force Aerial Refueling Tanker Replacement: Hearing before the House Committee on Armed Services, July 10, 2008; KC-X Tanker Recompete Act, H.R. 6426, 110th Congress, at § 2(a).

[4] Memorandum for Secretaries of the Military Departments, Chairman of the Joint Chiefs of Staff, Under Secretaries of Defense, Aug. 24, 2007, *available at* http://acquisition.navy.mil/rda/content/download/5263/23838/file/enhancing%20competition%201-18-2008.pdf (describing bid protests as "extremely detrimental to the warfighter and taxpayer" and stating that "[t]he Defense Department must take steps in an effort to avoid these protest situations").

[5] Duncan Hunter National Defense Authorization Act for Fiscal Year 2009: Report of the Committee on Armed Services, House of Representatives, on H.R. 5658, at 394-95 (2008).

[6] GAO, *Report to Congress on Bid Protests Involving Defense Procurements*, Apr. 9, 2009, *available at* http://www.gao.gov/decisions/bidpro/401197.pdf.

[7] *See, e.g.*, Industry's Wish List for Procurement Reform, *Wash. Tech.*, Nov. 20, 2009, *available at* http://washingtontechnology.com/blogs/editors-notebook/2009/11/gordon-ofpp-wish-list.aspx (listing "address[ing] the growing number of contract protests" as one of industry's top wishes); TSA Infrastructure Contract Enters the Ridiculous Zone, *Wash. Tech.*, Nov. 19, 2009, *available at* http://washingtontechnology.com/blogs/editors-notebook/ 2009/11/tsa-

stops-work-again.aspx (describing how work on one particular contract was started, stopped, resumed, and stopped a second time due to protest activity).

[8] For more on the GAO generally, see CRS Report RL30349, *GAO: Government Accountability Office and General Accounting Office*, by Frederick M. Kaiser.

[9] 31 U.S.C. § 3551(1)(A)-(D).

[10] The Budget and Accounting Act of 1921, P.L. 67-13, § 305, 42 Stat. 20, 24 (June 10, 1921).

[11] 310 U.S. 113, 132 (1940).

[12] *Id.* at 127.

[13] Congress passed the APA in 1946, but it was not until 1970 that the federal courts held that the APA gave them jurisdiction to hear bid protests. *See* Scanwell Labs., Inc. v. Schafer, 424 F.2d 859, 865-69 (D.C. Cir. 1970).

[14] CICA was enacted as part of the Deficit Reduction Act of 1984, P.L. 98-369, §§ 2701-2753, 98 Stat. 1175 (1984) (codified, in part, at 31 U.S.C. § 3556). Certain specific issues relating to the award of federal contracts are to be protested to other agencies, rather than the bid-protest forums. Size certification determinations for small businesses, for example, are to be protested with the Small Business Administration. *See* 13 C.F.R. § 121.1001.

[15] 31 U.S.C. § 3554(a)(1).

[16] *Compare* 31 U.S.C. § 3554(a)(1) (establishing 100-day timeframe for GAO decision) *with* 4 C.F.R. § 21.2(a)(2) (establishing that protests must generally be filed within 10 days after the basis for protesting was known or should have been known).

[17] A protest is, by definition, a written objection. 31 U.S.C. § 3551(1).

[18] 31 U.S.C. § 3551(1)(A)-(D).

[19] *See Bid Protest Annual Report, supra* note 1.

[20] These issues are generally protested with the Small Business Administration (SBA). For more information on the 8(a) Program, see CRS Report R40744, *The "8(a) Program" for Small Businesses Owned and Controlled by the Socially and Economically Disadvantaged: Legal Requirements and Issues*, by John R. Luckey and Kate M. Manuel.

[21] Such violations include the release of source selection information or contractor bid or proposal information by the agency; undisclosed contacts between employees involved in procurements over $100,000 and bidders or offerors regarding future employment; or employment by the contractor of former agency officials who were involved in procurements or administration of contracts valued at $10 million or more within one year of their involvement. *See* 41 U.S.C. § 423.

[22] P.L. 81-152, 63 Stat. 377 (1949). Examples of such agencies include the U.S. Postal Service and the Federal Deposit Insurance Corporation.

[23] An agency can agree in writing to have other protests—known as non-statutory protests—decided by GAO. 4 C.F.R. § 21.13(a).

[24] For more on debarment and suspension, see CRS Report RL34753, *Debarment and Suspension of Government Contractors: An Overview of the Law Including Recently Enacted and Proposed Amendments*, by Kate M. Manuel.

[25] 4 C.F.R. § 21.5(a)-(k). For more on public-private competitions, see CRS Report RL32833, *Competitive Sourcing Statutes and Statutory Provisions*, by L. Elaine Halchin.

[26] 31 U.S.C. § 3553(a).

[27] 31 U.S.C. § 3551(2)(A).

[28] GAO, Office of General Counsel, *Bid Protests at GAO: A Descriptive Guide* 5 (8th ed. 2006), *available at* http://meetings.abanet.org/webupload/commupload/PC402000/relatedresources/GAOGuidetoBidProtests(EighthEditiionMay2006).pdf.

[29] *See, e.g.*, Arora Group, B-288127 (Comp. Gen. Sept. 14, 2001) (recognizing a bidder whose proposal was ranked fifth as an interested party only because its protest challenged the agency's application of the evaluation criteria in general and, if successful, could have placed the contractor in line for the award).

[30] 4 C.F.R. § 21.0(b)(1).

[31] *Id.*
[32] 4 C.F.R. § 21.1(f).
[33] 4 C.F.R. § 21.4(c)(1)-(8).
[34] 4 C.F.R. § 21.1(d)(1)-(3).
[35] *Bid Protests at GAO, supra* note 28, at 3. However, only attorneys admitted under protective orders are permitted to see another company's proprietary information, or the agency's source-selection-sensitive information, during a GAO protest. *Id.* at 5-6.
[36] 4 C.F.R. § 21.7(a) (allowing parties to a bid protest to request a hearing). *See also* 4 C.F.R. § 21.7(c) (noting that, although hearings are generally conducted in Washington, D.C., they can sometimes be conducted in other locations, by telephone, or by other electronic means).
[37] *Bid Protest Annual Report, supra* note 1.
[38] 4 C.F.R. § 21.7(b).
[39] Robert S. Metzger & Daniel A. Lyons, A Critical Reassessment of the GAO Bid-Protest Mechanism, 6 *Wis. L. Rev.* 1225, 1232 (2007).
[40] *Id.*
[41] *Id.* at 1241.
[42] *Bid Protests at GAO, supra* note 28, at 7.
[43] Metzger & Lyons, *supra* note 39, at 1232. In many cases, judges on the Court of Federal Claims hold some sort of hearing on the merits within 60 to 90 days of the protest's filing. The court does not always render its decision at the same time as the hearing, however. The decision could come weeks or months later.
[44] 4 C.F.R. § 21.2(a)(1). When the alleged improprieties did not exist in the initial solicitation, but were subsequently incorporated into it, the protest must be filed prior to the next closing time for receipt of proposals following the incorporation. *Id.*
[45] 4 C.F.R. § 21.2(a)(2). A debriefing is a meeting between unsuccessful bidders or offerors and agency officials wherein agency officials explain why the proposal of the bidder or offeror was not selected. When contractors protest with the GAO after an earlier protest with the contracting agency, that protest must also be filed with GAO within 10 calendar days of the agency's denying this protest unless the agency had set a shorter timeframe for protesters' "appeal" of agency decisions to GAO. 4 C.F.R. § 21.2(a)(3).
[46] 4 C.F.R. § 21.2(b)-(c).
[47] 4 C.F.R. § 21.2(c).
[48] 28 U.S.C. § 2401(a).
[49] 31 U.S.C. § 3553(b)(1). The protester must also submit a copy of the protest to the agency within one working day of filing the protest with GAO. 4 C.F.R. § 21.1(e).
[50] 31 U.S.C. § 3553(c)(1) & (d)(1).
[51] 31 U.S.C. § 3553(b)(2)(A). This 30-day response period can be lengthened when the Comptroller General determines, based upon the agency's written request, that the circumstances of the protest require a longer period. 31 U.S.C. § 3553(b)(2)(B). The response period can also be shortened to 20 days when the Comptroller General determines that the protest is suitable for "express" resolution and notifies the agency of this determination. 31 U.S.C. § 3553(b)(2)(C).
[52] 31 U.S.C. § 3553(b)(2)(A).
[53] 4 C.F.R. § 21.3(c).
[54] 4 C.F.R. § 21.3(b).
[55] 4 C.F.R. § 21.3(i). In protests decided under the "express option," this timeframe is reduced to five days. 4 C.F.R. § 21.10(d).
[56] 4 C.F.R. § 21.3(i).
[57] 31 U.S.C. § 3554(a)(1). GAO must also resolve timely supplemental or amended protests within this timeframe, if possible. 4 C.F.R. § 21.9(c).
[58] 31 U.S.C. § 3554(a)(2); 4 C.F.R. § 21.10.
[59] 31 U.S.C. § 3554(a)(4).
[60] 31 U.S.C. § 3553(b)(3).

[61] 4 C.F.R. § 21.10(e).
[62] 4 C.F.R. § 21.10(c).
[63] *Bid Protests at GAO*, *supra* note 28, at 20.
[64] 4 C.F.R. § 21.3(g).
[65] 4 C.F.R. § 21.7(g). If the protester fails to timely file these comments, GAO must, under its own regulations, dismiss the protest.
[66] 31 U.S.C. § 3553(c)(1).
[67] 31 U.S.C. § 3553(d)(1).
[68] *Id.*
[69] *See, e.g.*, PGBA, LLC v. United States, 57 Fed. Cl. 655, 657 (2003) (describing the stays as central to the GAO bid protest process).
[70] *See, e.g.*, *Competition in Contracting Act of 1984: H.R. Rep. No. 1157, 98th Cong., 2d Sess.* 24-25 (1984) (explaining that, prior to CICA, many agencies would proceed with the award during the protest, making the GAO's decision irrelevant in the face of a contractual *fait accompli*).
[71] A temporary restraining order bars a party to litigation from taking certain action(s) while the court decides to issue a preliminary injunction. In deciding whether to issue a temporary restraining order or a preliminary injunction, the Court of Federal Claims applies the same four-part test, looking at (1) whether the plaintiff is likely to succeed on the merits of the case, (2) whether the plaintiff will suffer irreparable harm if the court withholds the requested relief, (3) whether the balance of hardships to the parties favors the grant of the requested relief, and (4) whether it is in the public interest to grant the requested relief. *See, e.g.*, Career Training Concepts, Inc. v. United States, 83 Fed. Cl. 215, 218 (2008).
[72] Metzger & Lyons, *supra* note 39, at 1239. A disappointed bidder or offeror who is the incumbent contractor could obtain another 100 days worth of business from the agency by filing a protest with the GAO because agencies often continue incumbent contractors during the pendency of GAO protests. *See* 31 U.S.C. § 3553(d)(3)(C); *see also* Keeton Corrections, Inc. v. United States, 59 Fed. Cl. 753 (2004) (overruling the Bureau of Prisons' override of a CICA stay because the incumbent contractor could continue to provide correction services during the protest). Alternately, a disappointed bidder or offeror who is not the incumbent contractor could obtain temporary contracts with the agency during the protest.
[73] *Id.* at 1269.
[74] 31 U.S.C. § 3553(c)(1) & (d)(3). *See* Ameron, Inc. v. U.S. Army Corp. of Eng'rs, 607 F. Supp. 962, 974 (D.N.J. 1985) (describing the override as a "built-in safety value to prevent undue harm" to the government).
[75] 31 U.S.C. § 3553(c)(2)(A) & (d)(3)(C)(II).
[76] 31 U.S.C. § 3553(d)(3)(C)(II).
[77] 31 U.S.C. § 3553(c)(2).
[78] 31 U.S.C. § 3553(c) & (d).
[79] The key determinant of the agency's success in invoking either grounds for overriding a CICA stay is the agency's record of the procurement and its decision making. The agency must be able to demonstrate that its override determination was not arbitrary, capricious, or an abuse of discretion based upon the evidence in the record before it at the time the determination was made. *See, e.g.*, Protection Strategies, Inc. v. United States, 76 Fed. Cl. 225, 233-34 (2007) (discussing reviewing courts' focus upon agency records as they existed at the time of the override determination); U.S. Army Acquisition Corps, *CICA Automatic Stay Override Guide* 2 (2004), *available at* http:// http://www.aca.army.mil/docs/Community/aca_ovrid_gd.doc (suggesting that agency contracting officers should prepare their files so as to have strong records for judicial scrutiny).
[80] Robert M. Hansen, CICA Without Enforcement: How Procurement Officials and Federal Court Decisions Are Undercutting Enforcement Provisions of the Competition in Contracting Act, 6 *Geo. Mason L. Rev.* 131, 155 (1997) ("If an action is in the 'best interest

of the United States,' it certainly must be 'urgent and compelling,' and if it is 'urgent and compelling,' it very likely will be in the country's 'best interest.'").

[81] 31 U.S.C. § 3553(c)(1) & (d)(3).

[82] *Compare* GAO, *GAO Bid Protest Annual Report to the Congress for Fiscal Year 2003*, Jan. 30, 2004, *available at* http://www.gao.gov/special.pubs/bidpro03.pdf (not reporting on agency override determinations) *with* GAO, *GAO Bid Protest Annual Report to the Congress for Fiscal Year 2002*, Jan. 29, 2003, *available at* http://www.gao.gov/special.pubs/bidpro02.pdf (reporting on agency override determinations).

[83] Since *Ramcor Services Group, Inc. v. United States*, 183 F.3d 1286 (Fed. Cir. 1999), all such suits have been brought in the Court of Federal Claims.

[84] Because the case comes to the court on a motion for a temporary restraining order or preliminary injunction, the court applies its customary test, examining (1) whether the protester is likely to succeed on the merits, (2) whether the protester will suffer irreparable harm if the court denies the requested relief, (3) whether the balance of hardships favors the grant of the requested relief, and (4) whether the requested relief would further the public interest. *See, e.g.*, Career Training Concepts, 83 Fed. Cl. at 218. The court's analysis of whether the protester is likely to succeed on the merits, in turn, focuses upon whether the agency's override determination was "arbitrary, capricious, an abuse of discretion, or otherwise not in accordance with the law" in violation of the Administrative Procedure Act (APA). *See* 5 U.S.C. § 706(2)(A) (scope of review under the APA); Superior Helicopter LLC v. United States, 78 Fed. Cl. 181, 186-87 (2007) (application of APA to agency overrides). In this analysis, the court focuses upon whether significant adverse consequences would have resulted if the agency had not overridden the stay; whether the agency had reasonable alternatives to the override; how the benefits of the override compare to its potential costs, including the possibility that the protester might prevail in the GAO bid protest; and the impact of the override on competition and the integrity of the procurement system. *See, e.g.*, Reilly's Wholesale Produce, Inc. v. United States, 73 Fed. Cl. 705, 711 (2006).

[85] Topgallant Group, Inc. v. United States, 704 F. Supp. 265, 266 (D.D.C. 1988) (holding that determination of what is in the "best interests of the United States" is committed to agency discretion and unreviewable). *Topgallant* was followed by *SDS International, Inc. v. United States*, 55 Fed. Cl. 363 (2003); *Dairy Maid Dairy, Inc. v. United States*, 837 F. Supp. 1370 (E.D. Va. 1993); and other federal court decisions. The Court of Federal Claims rejected the logic of *Topgallant* shortly after its *SDS International* decision in *PGBA, Inc.*

[86] *See, e.g.*, Mark Dunning Indus., Inc. v. Perry, 890 F. Supp. 1504, 1511 (M.D. Ala. 1995) (stating that courts are to apply a particularly deferential standard of review in determining agency rationality in override determinations); Stay, Inc. v. Cheney, 940 F.2d 1457, 1463 (11th Cir. 1991) (same).

[87] The standard of "searching inquiry" is that from *Citizens to Preserve Overton Park v. Volpe*, 41 U.S. 402, 416 (1971). Commentators have noted that the Court of Federal Claims has been less deferential to agency override determinations since 2006, when it issued its decision in *Reilly's Wholesale Produce*. *See, e.g.*, Kevin J. Wilkinson & Dennis C. Ehlers, Ensuring CICA Stay Overrides Are Reasonable, Supportable, and Less Vulnerable to Attack: Practical Recommendations in Light of Recent COFC Cases, 60 *A.F. L. Rev.* 91, 93 (2006) (describing 2006 as a "watershed" year).

[88] *See, e.g.*, SDS Int'l, 55 Fed. Cl. at 366 (stating that courts must give "due regard" to the interests of national defense and national security when deciding bid protests); Maden Tech Consulting Inc. v. United States, 74 Fed. Cl. 786, 790 (2006) ("Where legitimate 'interests of national defense and national security' [are] asserted and established to the court's satisfaction, the court will not 'reach the merits of whether [CICA] is violated.'").

[89] *Compare* Gentex Corp. v. United States, 58 Fed. Cl. 634, 655-56 (2003) (stating that assertions of national security and national defense get more deference but the court still examines their merits) *and* Geo-Seis Helicopters, Inc. v. United States, 77 Fed. Cl. 633, 650 (2007)

(focusing upon national security concerns in tailoring injunctive relief, not in deciding on the merits of the case) *with* Hughes Missile Sys. Co. v. Dep't of Air Force, No. 96-937, slip. op. at 77 (E.D. Va. 1996), quoted in Hansen, *supra* note 80, at 154, (upholding an agency's override without reaching the merits of the plaintiff's argument even though the agency conceded that it prepared its findings justifying the override determination after the fact).

[90] 31 U.S.C. § 3552(a).

[91] *See, e.g.*, Baker Support Sys., B-257054.2 (Comp. Gen. Jan. 20, 1995).

[92] *See, e.g.*, 31 U.S.C. § 3552(a) (agency compliance with statutes and regulations); McWane & Co., B-280374 (Comp. Gen. Mar. 1, 1996) (agency evaluation's having a reasonable basis and being consistent with evaluation criteria in the request for proposals); Moheat Env. Servs., B-270538 (Comp. Gen. Nov. 20, 1996) (agency evaluation's having a reasonable basis and adequate documentation even if otherwise inconsistent with the evaluation criteria).

[93] 31 U.S.C. § 3554(b)(1)(A)-(G).

[94] 4 C.F.R. § 21.8(b).

[95] *Id.*

[96] *See* Ameron, Inc. v. United States Army Corps of Eng'gs, 809 F.2d 979, 986 (3d Cir. 1986).

[97] 31 U.S.C. § 3554(c)(1)(A)-(B). The Court of Federal Claims, in contrast, has ruled that it does not have jurisdiction over bid protest costs. S.K.J. & Assocs. v. United States, 67 Fed. Cl. 218 (2005).

[98] 31 U.S.C. § 3554(c)(3)(A)-(B). Where GAO recommends fees for consultants, expert witnesses, or attorneys, no party other than a small business concern within the meaning of Section 3(a) of the Small Business Act may be paid costs for consultant- or expert-witness-fees that exceed the highest rate of compensation for expert witnesses paid by the federal government, or costs for attorneys' fees that exceed $150 per hour, unless the agency determines that an increase in the cost of living or a special factor justifies a higher fee. 31 U.S.C. § 3554(c)(2)(A)-(B).

[99] 31 U.S.C. § 3554(c)(4).

[100] *Id.*

[101] Metzger & Lyons, *supra* note 39, at 1232, 1248. GAO, in contrast, will not hear protests that have been the subject of litigation or have been decided on the merits by a court of competent jurisdiction. 4 C.F.R. § 21.11(b).

[102] 31 U.S.C. § 3554(b)(3).

[103] B-400278; B-400308, 2008 U.S. Comp. Gen. LEXIS 193 (September 19, 2008).

[104] Mission Critical Solutions, B-410057, 2009 U.S. Comp. Gen. LEXIS 86 (May 4, 2009).

[105] For more on *International Program Group, Mission Critical Solutions*, and the executive branch's response, see CRS Report R40591, *Set-Asides for Small Businesses: Recent Developments in the Law Regarding Precedence Among the Set-Aside Programs and Set-Asides Under Indefinite-Delivery/Indefinite-Quantity Contracts*, by Kate M. Manuel.

[106] *See* Executive Office of the President, Office of Mgmt. & Budget, Recent Government Accountability Office Decisions Concerning Small Business Programs, July 10, 2009, *available at* http://www.whitehouse.gov/omb/assets/memoranda_fy2009/m09-23.pdf (directing agencies not to give HUBZone set-asides precedence over set-asides for service-disabled veteran-owned and 8(a) small businesses until OMB instructs otherwise); Office of Legal Counsel, Department of Justice, Permissibility of Small Business Administration Regulations Implementing the Historically Underutilized Business Zone, 8(a) Business Development, and Service-Disabled Veteran-Owned Small Business Concern Programs, Aug. 21, 2009, available at http://www.usdoj.gov/olc/2009/sba-hubzone-opinion082109.pdf (disagreeing with GAO and finding that Small Business Administration regulations, which provide for parity, not precedence, among the set-aside programs, constitute a reasonable interpretation of the Small Business Act entitled to deference under *Chevron U.S.A., Inc. v. Natural Resources Defense Council, Inc.*).

[107] Mission Critical Solutions v. United States, 2010 U.S. Claims LEXIS *36 (Mar. 2, 2010).

[108] 31 U.S.C. § 3554(b)(3). The agency has five calendar days after the end of the 60-day period to notify GAO. The congressional committees to which GAO reports this information are the Senate Committee on Homeland Security and Governmental Affairs, the Senate Committee on Appropriations, the House Committee on Oversight and Government Reform, and the House Committee on Appropriations. When notifying these congressional committees, GAO must provide a comprehensive review of the challenged procurement and a recommendation as to whether Congress should consider (1) private relief legislation, (2) legislative rescission or cancellation of funds, (3) further investigation by Congress, or (4) other action to correct an inequity or preserve the integrity of the procurement process. 31 U.S.C. § 3554(e)(1)(A)-(B). GAO must also submit an annual report to Congress including, among other things, a summary of each instance in which an agency did not fully implement a GAO recommendation. 31 U.S.C. § 3554(e)(2).

[109] *See, e.g.*, Jason Miller, OPM Blinks, Revisits USAJobs Buy, *Gov't Computer News*, Apr. 19, 2004, *available at* http://mobile.gcn.com/articles/23_8/25609-1.html (reporting that the chairman of the House Government Reform Committee threatened the Office of Personnel Management (OPM) with loss of funding for the project after OPM failed to adopt GAO's recommendation to re-compete the contract).

[110] *Geo-Seis Helicopters*, 77 Fed. Cl. at 636-38 (Fed. Cl. 2007). FAR Section 52.215-1(c)(3)(ii)(A) says that "[a]ny proposal, modification, or revision, received at the Government office designated in the solicitation after the exact time specified for receipt of offers is 'late' and will not be considered.").

[111] 77 Fed. Cl. at 638.

[112] *Id.* at 646.

[113] Grunley Walsh Int'l, LLC v. United States, 78 Fed. Cl. 35, 37-38 (Fed. Cl. 2007).

[114] *Id.*

[115] *Id.*

[116] *Id.* at 44.

[117] *See, e.g.*, Transatlantic Lines LLC v. United States, 68 Fed. Cl. 48 (2005) (finding for the protester after the GAO had denied the protest); Blue DOT Energy Co. v. United States, 76 Fed. Cl. 783 (2004) (same).

[118] Prior cases tended to avoid language suggesting agency "violations" of the APA even when finding such violations in their analysis of the merits of the protest. *See, e.g.*, Arora Group, Inc. v. United States, 2004 US Claims LEXIS 267 (Aug. 31, 2004) (using the protester's language, which mentioned "violations" of the APA, only when stating the plaintiff's allegations and not when deciding the merits of the case).

[119] 4 C.F.R. § 21.14(a).

[120] 4 C.F.R. § 21.14(b).

[121] 4 C.F.R. § 21.14(a).

[122] 4 C.F.R. § 21.14(c).

[123] *Id.*

[124] *See, e.g.*, Jerome S. Gabig, Jr., Fighting over Government Contracts, 66 *Ala. L. Rev.* 39, 42 (2005).

[125] 5 U.S.C. § 706(2)(A); Superior Helicopter LLC, 78 Fed. Cl. at 186-87 (application of APA to agency procurement activities). Not all bid protests in the Court of Federal Claims following GAO protests directly "appeal" GAO decisions, however. In some cases, the protester makes a different argument in the Court of Federal Claims than it made at GAO. *See, e.g.*, J&H Reinforcing & Structural Erectors, Inc. v. United States, 50 Fed. Cl. 570 (2001). In other cases, the GAO protest ended without a decision on merits from GAO. *See, e.g.*, Ezenia!, Inc. v. United States, 80 Fed. Cl. 60 (2007) (protester withdrew its GAO protest after filing suit in the Court of Federal Claims); Heritage of Am., LLC v. United States, 77 Fed. Cl. 66 (2007) (GAO protest dismissed as untimely).

[126] 31 U.S.C. § 3556. Parties to bid protests at the Court of Federal Claims are not strictly limited to the administrative record from the agency or GAO. They can move to supplement the

record, and the court will typically grant such motions when the "record does not contain sufficient information for the court to render a decision." Comp. Health Servs., Inc. v. United States, 70 Fed. Cl. 700, 720 (2006). This includes "fill[ing] gaps concerning the factors the contracting officer considered in reaching his decision." Precision Standard, Inc. v. United States, 69 Fed. Cl. 738, 745 (2006).

[127] *See, e.g.*, MTB Group v. United States, 65 Fed. Cl. 516 (2005). The Court of Federal Claims will affirm GAO on questions of fact, or questions that must be answered by facts and evidence, or inferences therefrom, unless the GAO decision is arbitrary, capricious, or so grossly erroneous as to imply bad faith. However, on questions of law, or questions that must be answered by applying relevant legal principles, the Court of Federal Claims gives no deference to GAO and conducts *de novo* review. Because most bid protests do not hinge upon factual questions, this means that most Court of Federal Claims decisions entail independent determinations on the legality of agency contracting activities.

[128] Bendix Field Eng'g Corp. v. United States, 1991 U.S. Dist. LEXIS 19778, at *6 (D.D.C. Nov. 15, 1991).

[129] Impresa Construzioni Geom. Domenico Garufi v. United States, 238 F.3d 1324, 1332 (Fed. Cir. 2001).

[130] Alion Science & Tech. Corp. v. United States, 69 Fed. Cl. 14, 25 (2005) (quoting Motor Vehicle Mfrs. Ass'n of the United States v. State Farm Ins. Co., 463 U.S. 29, 43 (1983).

In: Government Awards and Objections: Bid... ISBN: 978-1-61728-680-3
Editor: Matthew A. Sauter

Chapter 2

GAO BID PROTESTS: TRENDS, ANALYSIS, AND OPTIONS FOR CONGRESS*

Moshe Schwartz and Kate M. Manuel

SUMMARY

Bid protests filed with the Government Accountability Office (GAO) have recently received increased congressional scrutiny due to protests of high-profile awards and reports that the number of protests is increasing. The delay of contract award or performance triggered by a GAO protest, coupled with the increasing number of GAO protests, has also prompted concerns about the potential impact of protests upon government agency operations, especially in the Department of Defense.

GAO is one of three forums with authority to hear general bid protests against the government. The GAO's bid-protest process includes some unique features—most notably, the automatic stay of contract award or performance during a GAO protest—that make GAO a desirable forum for many disappointed bidders and offerors.

In recent years, the number of protests filed with GAO has steadily increased. Excluding protests from expanded jurisdiction, the number of bid

* This is an edited, reformatted and augmented version of a CRS Report for Congress publication dated February 2010.

protests increased steadily from approximately 1,150 in Fiscal Year (FY) 2001 to over 1,550 in FY2008, an increase of 37%. However, most of these protests were dismissed, withdrawn by the protester, or settled prior to GAO issuing an opinion. Since FY2001, on average, GAO issued an opinion on only 22% of bid protests; on average, GAO opinions sustained the protest approximately 20% of the time.

From FY2001 to FY2008, on average 5% of bid protests were sustained; neither the number—nor percentage—of protests sustained during the period increased significantly. In FY2001, GAO sustained 66 protests, or 6% of all protests. In FY2008, GAO sustained 60 protests, or 4% of all protests filed, despite a 37% increase in the number of bid protests filed over the same period. According to GAO officials, among the most common grounds for sustaining protests are the contracting agencies not maintaining adequate documentation, errors in how agency officials conduct discussions with offerors, flaws in cost evaluations, and contracting agencies not adhering to established evaluation criteria.

Protesters can obtain relief from a protest when GAO sustains a protest or when agencies voluntary act to correct the allegation charged in the protest. The percentage of protesters obtaining relief from an agency is called the effectiveness rate. The effectiveness rate may be a good way to measure the number of protests that have actual or potential merit. From FY2001 to FY2008, the effectiveness rate of GAO protests gradually increased from 33% to 42%, respectively. The increase in the effectiveness rate could indicate that not only are the number of protests increasing but the number of protests that have merit is increasing.

The number of bid protests filed against the Department of Defense (DOD) consistently increased, from approximately 600 in FY2001 to approximately 840 in FY2008, an increase of 38%. During the same period, on average, 60% of all bid protests involved DOD contracts even though DOD accounted for an average of 68% of all federal spending. From FY2001 to FY2008, neither the number—nor percentage—of bid protests sustained against DOD has consistently increased. According to data provided by GAO, protests against DOD were not sustained at a higher rate than the rest of government.

This chapter contains options for Congress related to minimizing the number of protests filed with GAO and the delay of award/execution often associated with protests being sustained.

INTRODUCTION

Bid protests filed with the Government Accountability Office (GAO), have received increased congressional scrutiny due to recent protests of high-profile awards reports and reports that the number of protests is increasing. 1 On December 22, 2008, the GAO notified Congress that it received 1,652 protests in FY2008, a 17% increase over the number of filings in Fiscal Year (FY) 2007.2 Some of these protests involved high-profile procurements—such as the Air Force's aerial refueling tankers, and combat, search, and rescue (CSAR-X) helicopters.3 In one case, the 110th Congress held hearings on a protested procurement and considered legislation that would have precluded government agencies from making a contested award.4 Additionally, the increasing number of protests filed with GAO, and the impact protests have in delaying contract award or performance, have raised concerns regarding the impact of protests on agency operations, especially in the Department of Defense (DOD). John J. Young, Jr., then Acting Under Secretary of Defense for Acquisition, Technology and Logistics, issued a memorandum in August 2007 in which he described bid protests as "extremely detrimental to the warfighter and taxpayer," and said that "[t]he Defense Department must take steps in an effort to avoid these protest situations."5 Partly in response to such concerns, the House Armed Services Committee, in authorizing DOD's budget for FY2009, requested that GAO investigate and report on the impact of bid protests on DOD.6

This chapter is one of two providing Congress with background on the GAO bid-protest process. It analyzes (1) trends in bid protests filed with GAO, (2) the impact bid protests have in delaying contracts, (3) the most common grounds for GAO to sustain a protest, and (4) trends in bid protests filed against DOD. Its companion report, CRS Report R40228, GAO Bid Protests: An Overview of Timeframes and Procedures, by Kate M. Manuel and Moshe Schwartz, provides an overview of the GAO bid protest process, including (1) what issues can be protested, (2) who can file or be a party to a protest, (3) the procedures for bringing and resolving protests, (4) the timeframes involved in protests, (5) the automatic stay of contract award or performance triggered by a protest, as well as the basis for agency overrides of automatic stays and judicial review of agency override determinations, (6) the basis and effects of GAO decisions, and (7) reconsideration and "appeal" of decisions.7

BACKGROUND

The foundation of today's federal procurement system dates back to the Armed Services Procurement Act of 1947 and the Federal Property and Administration Act of 1949.[8] The two post World War II acts, as amended, particularly by the Competition in Contracting Act of 1984, along with the Federal Acquisition Regulation (FAR), constitute most of today's federal procurement system.[9] The FAR, first published in 1984, regulates how the federal government acquires goods and services by codifying uniform policies and procedures for the entire executive branch.[10] The intent of the FAR is to help guide the Federal Acquisition System to "deliver on a timely basis the best value product or service to the [government], while maintaining the public's trust and fulfilling public policy objectives."[11]

One of the guiding principles of the FAR is to promote competition for government contracts.12 Competition has been an integral part of the federal procurement system since 1781, when the then Superintendent of Finance conducted the first formal open competition by advertising in a local newspaper for contract proposals to provide food for federal employees in Philadelphia.13 Many of the same principles that held true for the competition in 1781 hold true today.

Today, the federal acquisition process generally begins when an agency determines that it needs a good or service, and that the appropriate method for procuring the good or service is to contract with a private company. For contracts valued in excess of $100,000, an agency generally develops a solicitation identifying what the agency wants to buy, advertises the solicitation, identifies the method for evaluating offers, and sets a deadline for the submission of bids or proposals. The agency then evaluates the bids or proposals based on the criteria set forth in the solicitation and awards a contract to the winning firm.[14]

In an effort to protect the integrity of the procurement system, the FAR and federal law provide mechanisms for contractors to object to contract awards. Generally, any interested party15 who believes that a contract has been awarded unlawfully can seek relief and contest the award by filing a bid protest.16 The Government Accountability Office has been a forum for resolving bid protest disputes for more than 80 years. Historically, however, an interested party could file a protest in a number of forums, including the General Services Board of Contract Appeals and the U.S. District Court. By 2001, Congress had removed bid protest jurisdiction from the General Services Board of Contract Appeals and the U.S. District Court, leaving GAO the sole government-wide forum for hearing administrative protests and the Court of Federal Claims (COFC) the only judicial forum for hearing such protests.17 Companies can also file a protest with the agency awarding the contract, and under certain circumstances, with specialized entities, such as the Small Business Administration or the Bureau of Indian Affairs.18 GAO, however, remains the primary forum for resolving government contract bid protests.19

GAO BID PROTESTS

GAO may generally hear protests alleging illegalities or improprieties in solicitations, cancellations of solicitations, or awards or proposed awards of contracts that are filed by interested parties. The procedures for bringing and conducting GAO protests are designed to ensure "the inexpensive and expeditious resolution of [bid] protests" to "the maximum extent practicable."20 Protesters need not file formal briefs or technical pleadings,21 can represent themselves,22 and can have protests decided without hearings.23 All protests are required to be resolved within 100 calendar days of being filed.24 The filing of a GAO protest often triggers an automatic stay of contract award or performance that can interrupt agencies' procurement initiatives for as long as the protest is pending.25

GAO may deny or sustain bid protests. A denial allows the agency to proceed with the challenged award. A sustained decision, in contrast, generally disrupts the proposed award because GAO accompanies sustainments with recommendations to the agency about the challenged award – such as re-competing the contract or issuing a new solicitation.26 GAO's recommendations are not legally binding upon the agency, but the agency must notify GAO if it does not fully implement GAO's recommendations.27 GAO is, in turn, required to inform Congress of any instances in which agencies do not fully implement GAO recommendations.28 Agencies generally comply with GAO recommendations on protested procurements.29 Protesters that are disappointed with GAO's decision can seek reconsideration from GAO.30 They can also effectively "appeal" GAO's decision by filing a new bid protest with the Court of Federal Claims.31 For more information regarding the GAO bid protest process, please see CRS companion report GAO Bid-Protests: An Overview of Its Timeframes and Procedures.

Number of Bid Protests Filed with GAO

As previously mentioned, GAO notified Congress that it received 1,652 protests in FY2008, a 17% increase over the number of filings in FY2007.[32] However, Congress expanded GAO's jurisdiction in FY2007 to include hearing protests on task orders, A-76 contracts, and Transportation Security Administration contracts.[33] The reported number of protests filed in FY2008 includes 87 bid protests filed as a result of the expanded jurisdiction.[34] Excluding protests from expanded jurisdiction, the number of protest in FY2008 increased 11% over the number of filings in FY2007. From FY2001 to FY2008, the number of bid protests filed steadily increased from approximately 1,150 to over 1,550, respectively, an increase of 37% (see **Figure 1**). Most protests are dismissed, withdrawn by the protester, or settled prior to GAO issuing an opinion. Since FY2001, on average, GAO issued an opinion on only 22% of bid protests. Of the opinions issued during this period, on average, GAO sustained the about 20% of the time. As a result, from FY2001 to FY2008, approximately 5% of all protests filed were sustained (see **Figure 1**).

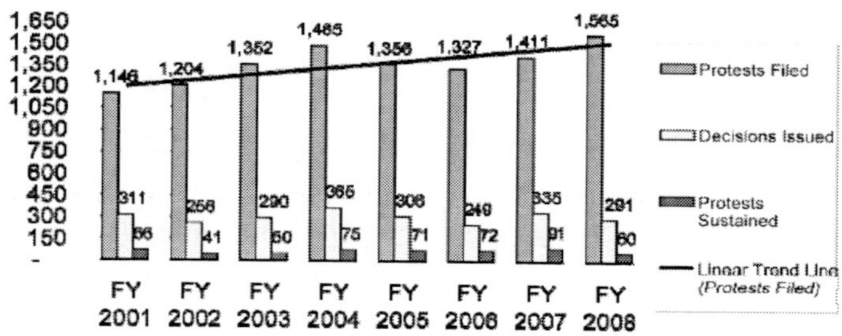

Source: CRS Analysis of Comptroller General annual reports to Congress for FY 2001 – FY 2008. See http://www.gao.gov/decisions/bidproan.htm for copies of the reports.

Notes: FY 2008 data exclude bid protests filed as a result of GAO's expanded jurisdiction over task orders (49 filings), A-76 protests (30 filings), and Transportation Security Administration protests (8 filings).

In statistical terms, the R^2 value for the linear trend line is 0.6418. R^2 is a statistical term used to describe the goodness of the fit between the trend line and the data points. R^2 is a descriptive measure between 0 and 1. The closer the R^2 value is to one, the better the fit of the trend line to the data.

Figure 1. Number of Bid Protests Filed With GAO (FY2001- FY2008)

In addition to GAO sustaining a protest, protesters can also obtain relief when a contracting agency voluntary acts to correct the allegation charged in the protest. Many analysts consider the increasing willingness of agencies to voluntarily take corrective action as one of the most significant trends in bid protests. Such voluntary action by an agency could indicate that the agency believes that a given protest has merit.

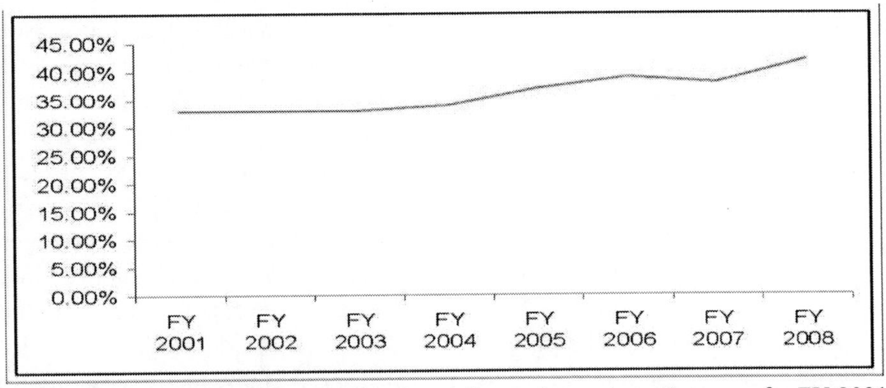

Source: CRS Analysis of Comptroller General annual reports to Congress for FY 2001 – FY 2008. See http://www.gao.gov/decisions/bidproan.htm for copies of the reports.

Notes: Based on a protester obtaining some form of relief from the agency, as reported to GAO.

Figure 2. Effectiveness Rate of GAO Protests (FY2001 – FY2008)

The percentage of protesters obtaining relief – either through a protest being sustained or through voluntary action taken by an agency—is called the effectiveness rate. The effectiveness rate may be a good way to measure the number of protests that have actual or potential merit. From FY2001 to FY2008, the effectiveness rate of GAO protests grew from 33% to 42%, respectively (see Figure **2**).[35] The increase in the effectiveness rate could indicate that not only are the number of protests increasing but the number of protests that have merit is also increasing.

Recent media reports discussing the increase in protests have fueled the debate over why the number of protests is rising.36 Some analysts may take the increase as evidence that the government's ability to properly award contracts is getting worse. Others may attribute the trend to an increasing willingness of companies to file protests. Such analysts might argue that the increase in value of individual contracts and longer periods of contract performance make contractors more desperate to win each contract—and more willing to protest an award.

The number—and value—of contract actions signed by the federal government has grown at a faster rate than the number of protests filed with GAO.37 According to USAspending.gov, between FY2001 and FY2008, the number of contract actions executed by the federal government increased by almost 600% and the value of those contracts increased over 100% (see Figures 3 & 4).38 Even after adjusting for inflation, federal contract spending increased by approximately 80% between FY2001 and FY2007.39 This compares to a 37% increase in the number of protests filed with the GAO. Even though the data reported in USASpending.gov does not correlate perfectly with the GAO data, some could argue that the trend in increased government contracting activity is clear—the recent rise in protests correlates to an increase in government contracting activity.40 Others can point out that since contract actions and spending have risen at a faster rate than protests, the proportion of contracts being protested has actually decreased. Put into historical context, the number of protests filed in FY2008 is still substantially lower than the number filed from FY1995 to FY1997 (see Figure 5).

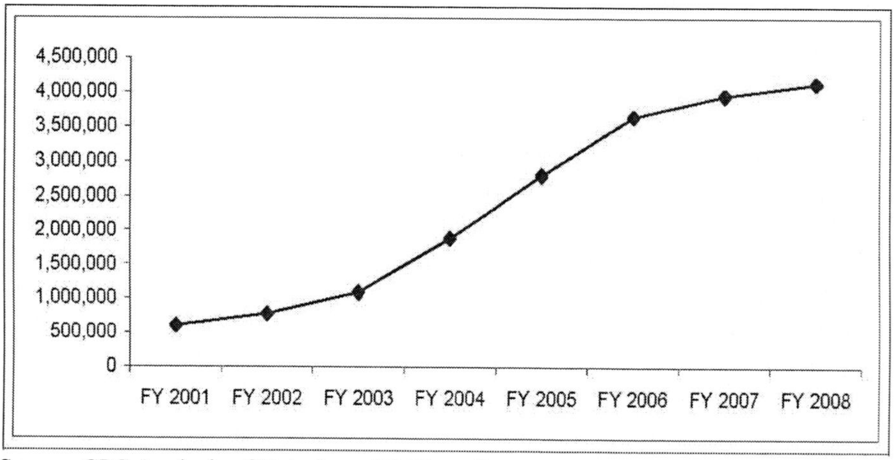

Source: CRS Analysis of Data from *USASpending.gov*.

Figure 3. Number of Federal Government Contract Actions FY2001 – FY2008

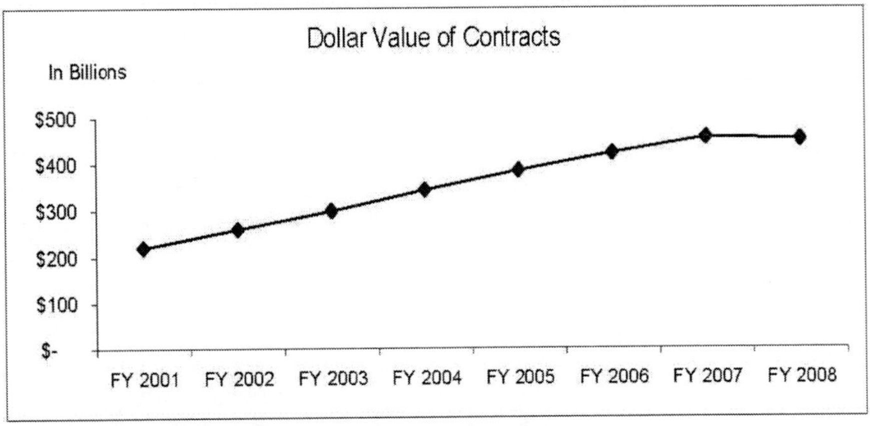

Source: CRS Analysis of Data from *USASpending.gov.*

Figure 4. Federal Contract Spending FY2001 – FY2008 (in Billions)

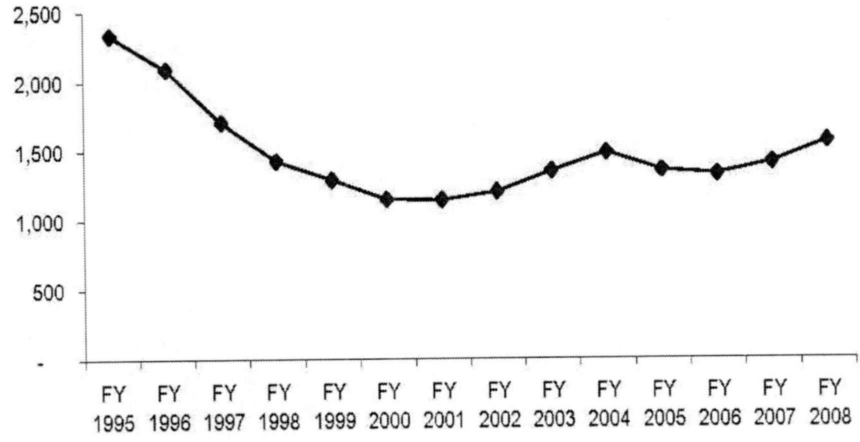

Source: CRS Analysis of Comptroller General annual reports to Congress for FY1996 – FY2008. See http://www.gao.gov/decisions/bidproan.htm for copies of the reports.

Notes: FY 2008 data excludes bid protests filed as a result of GAO's expanded jurisdiction over task orders (49 filings), A-76 protests (30 filings), and Transportation Security Administration protests (8 filings).

Figure 5. Number of Bid Protests Filed With GAO (FY1995 -FY2008)

Air Bid Protests Delaying Contracts?

Many analysts and acquisition professionals are concerned that bid protests can delay contract awards for weeks and even months, costing millions of dollars and preventing government from getting the goods and services it needs when it needs them. In an August 2007 memo, John Young, then Acting Under Secretary of Defense for Acquisition, Technology and Logistics, wrote that DOD

> has experienced a significant increase in the number of competitive source selection decisions which are protested by industry. Protests are extremely detrimental to the warfighter and the taxpayer. These protest actions consume vast amounts of the time of acquisition, legal, and requirements team members; delay program initiation and the delivery of capability....

A number of high-profile government acquisitions have experienced extensive delays as a result of GAO bid protest decisions. For example, on June 18, 2008, GAO sustained Boeing's protest of the Air Force's award of a contract to Northrop Grumman.[41] More than seven months later, a new Request for Proposal has not yet been issued. Identifying which protests tend to experience the longest delays—and working to minimize such delays—could help the government save hundreds of millions of dollars and receive the goods and services it needs when it needs them.

Bid Protests Trigger an Automatic Stay

Under the Competition in Contracting Act (CICA), the mere filing of a bid protest with GAO may trigger an automatic stay, or postponement, of contract award or performance.[42] When a protest is filed prior to award, an agency may not award a contested contract until the protest has been resolved.[43] Similarly, when a protest is filed after award, the agency must withhold authorization of performance under the contract while the protest is pending.[44] If authorization has not been withheld, the agency must "immediately direct the contractor to cease performance under the contract" until the protest is resolved.[45]

If an agency believes that circumstances are such that further delay in contract execution will have severe consequences, CICA provides grounds for agency overrides of automatic bid-protest stays.[46] According to CICA, agencies may override stays when there are "urgent and compelling circumstances" that impact the interests of the United States and when performing the contract is in "the best interests of the United States."[47] According to data provided by GAO, from FY2001 to FY2007 agencies sought to override CICA stays in over 650 contracts, or 7% of all protests filed during the period.[48]

GAO and the 100 Day Time Limit

GAO is required to complete its involvement in a protest within 100 calendar days of their filing.49 According to GAO officials, GAO has never failed to complete its work within the required time period. In many cases the protest is resolved much earlier.50 For example, a protest can have a shortened 65-calendar day deadline if the protest is treated under the "express option."51 GAO can also dismiss protests that do not meet filing guidelines within days of filing, and can issue a summary decision on a protest at any time.52 Since GAO completes its protest work within 100 days of a protest being filed, generally, any delay in contract award or execution that results from a GAO protest can be mitigated by starting the contracting process a few weeks earlier.

In FY2008, approximately 58% of all GAO protests were dismissed, withdrawn by the protester with no further action, or resolved in the agency's favor. Generally, for reasons discussed above, these protests delayed a contract for fewer than 100 days.

In FY2008, approximately 37% of all GAO bid protests were resolved based on the protestor obtaining some form of relief from the agency subsequent to filing a protest—but prior to GAO issuing an opinion. For example, an agency may recognize an error in the contracting process and choose to re-compete the contract. In these cases, protests are usually withdrawn as a result of the settlement between the parties or dismissed by GAO because the basis for the protest has been resolved. While the withdrawal or dismissal of these protests occurs within 100 days, it could take more than 100 days to provide relief. For example, if the agency agrees to re-compete a contract, the new competition could take more than 100 days. CRS was unable to obtain data on the extent to which such bid protests delay the award or execution of a contract.

Generally, protests sustained by GAO are most likely to delay contract award or execution. Developing a mechanism for remedying the problem more quickly may benefit the government. While on average only 5% of protests are sustained, many of these protests are controversial and receive significant media attention. For example, a recent article referring to the aerial refueling tanker (KC-X), Combat Search and Rescue Replacement helicopter (CSAR-X) and HUMVEES, stated "at least three major Pentagon programs worth a combined $70 billion were delayed this year due to protests filed by Boeing Co., Lockheed Martin Corp., and others."53

Number of Bid Protests Sustained by GAO

In recent years, neither the number—nor percentage—of bid protests sustained by GAO has increased significantly (see **Figures 6 & 7**). From FY2001 to FY2008, on average 5% of all protests filed were sustained. In FY2001, GAO sustained 66 protests, or 6% of all protests. In FY2008, GAO sustained 60 protests, or 4% of all protests filed, despite a 37% increase in the number of bid protests filed over the same period.

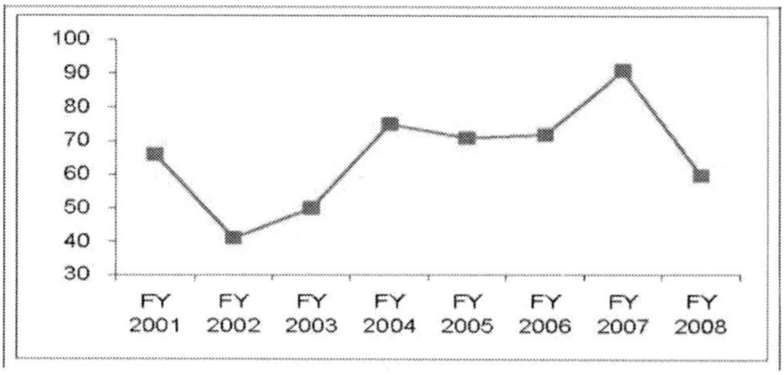

Source: CRS Analysis of Comptroller General annual reports to Congress for FY 2001 – FY 2008.

Note: The R^2 value for the linear trend line for the number of protests sustained during the period is 0.2578.

Figure 6. Number of Protests Sustained by GAO FY 2001 – FY 2008

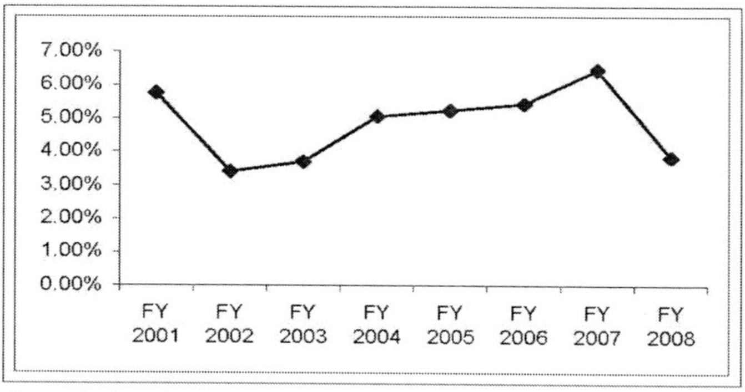

Source: CRS Analysis of Comptroller General annual reports to Congress for FY 2001 – FY 2008.

Note: The R^2 for the linear trend line for the percentage of protests sustained by GAO is 0.036.

Figure 7. Percentage of Protests Sustained by GAO FY 2001 – FY 2008

Common Grounds for GAO Sustaining Bid Protests

Knowing what aspect of the contracting process most often results in bid protests being sustained could help agencies focus on improving those aspects of contracting. Such improvements could help reduce the number of protests being filed and/or sustained.

GAO officials stated that they do not formally track the most common reasons protests are sustained.[54] Officials believe, however, that among the most common grounds for sustaining protests are

1. agencies not maintaining adequate documentation,
2. errors in how agency officials conduct discussions with offerors,
3. flaws in cost evaluations, and
4. agencies not adhering to established evaluation criteria.

For example, many of the common grounds for sustaining protests can be seen in GAO's decision to sustain Boeing's protest of the Air Force's award to Northrop Grumman for the aerial refueling tankers (KC-X).[55]

Documentation

Officials stated that there are strict statutory requirements for documenting agency decisions.56 In a number of cases, agencies failed to adhere to statutory requirements, resulting in GAO sustaining bid protests. For example, in the KC-X decision, GAO sustained the protest because "the record must contain adequate documentation showing the bases for the evaluation conclusions and source selection decision... Nevertheless, the record does not establish that the SSAC (Source Source Selection Advisory Council)Source Selection Authority (SSA) and SSA (Source Selection Authority), in considering those strengths and weaknesses, applied the relative weights identified in the RFP (Request for Proposal) for the various SRD (System Requirements Document) requirements (under which the KPPs [Key Performance Parameters] were most important). Moreover, the record does not show any consideration by the SSAC or SSA of the fact that Boeing's proposal was evaluated as satisfying significantly more SRD requirements than Northrop Grumman's."

Dontuct of Discussions with Offerors

Agencies sometimes conduct discussions with offerors in an unfair manner. For example, in the KC-X decision, GAO sustained the protest because "[t]he Air Force conducted misleading and unequal discussions with

Boeing, by informing Boeing that it had fully satisfied a key performance parameter...but later determined that Boeing had only partially met this objective, without advising Boeing of this change in the agency's assessment and while continuing to conduct discussions with Northrop Grumman...." Such unfair discussions are grounds for GAO sustaining a bid protest.

Cost Evaluations

Flaws in cost evaluation models result in bid protests being sustained. For example, in the KC-X decision, GAO sustained the protest because the Air Force's evaluation of construction costs in calculating Boeing's costs for their proposed aircraft was unreasonable. The Air Force conceded that it "made a number of errors in evaluation that, when corrected, result in Boeing displacing Northrop Grumman as the offeror with the lowest most probable life cycle cost...."

Failure to Adhere to Established Evaluation Criteria

Agencies do not always adhere to the evaluation criteria set forth in the Request for Proposal (RFP). For example, in the KC-X decision, GAO sustained the protest because "The Air Force, in making the award decision, did not assess the relative merits of the proposals in accordance with the evaluation criteria identified in the solicitation, which provided for a relative order of importance for the various technical requirements."

DOD Contracts and Bid Protests

The number of bid protests filed against DOD has increased from approximately 600 in FY2001 to approximately 840 in FY2008, an increase of 38% (see Figure 8). Most of the protests filed against DOD were dismissed, withdrawn by the protester, or settled prior to GAO issuing an opinion. In FY2008, GAO issued an opinion on 29% of these bid protests.57 Fewer still are sustained by GAO. From FY2001 to FY2008, on average only 5% of protests filed against DOD were sustained by GAO (see Table A-1 for number of protests filed and sustained, by service).

The overall dollar value of DOD contracts has increased proportionally more than the number of protests filed with GAO. According to USAspending.gov, between FY2001 and FY2008, the value of contracts actions signed by DOD increased by 120% (see Figure 9). Adjusting for inflation, federal contract spending increased more than 80% between FY2001 and FY2008.58 This compares to a 39% increase in the number of protests filed against DOD in the same period.59

In recent years, neither the number – nor percentage – of bid protests sustained against DOD has consistently increased (see **Table A-2**). In FY2001, GAO sustained 40 protests, or 7% of protests filed against DOD, compared to 30 protests, or 4% of protests filed against DOD in FY2008.

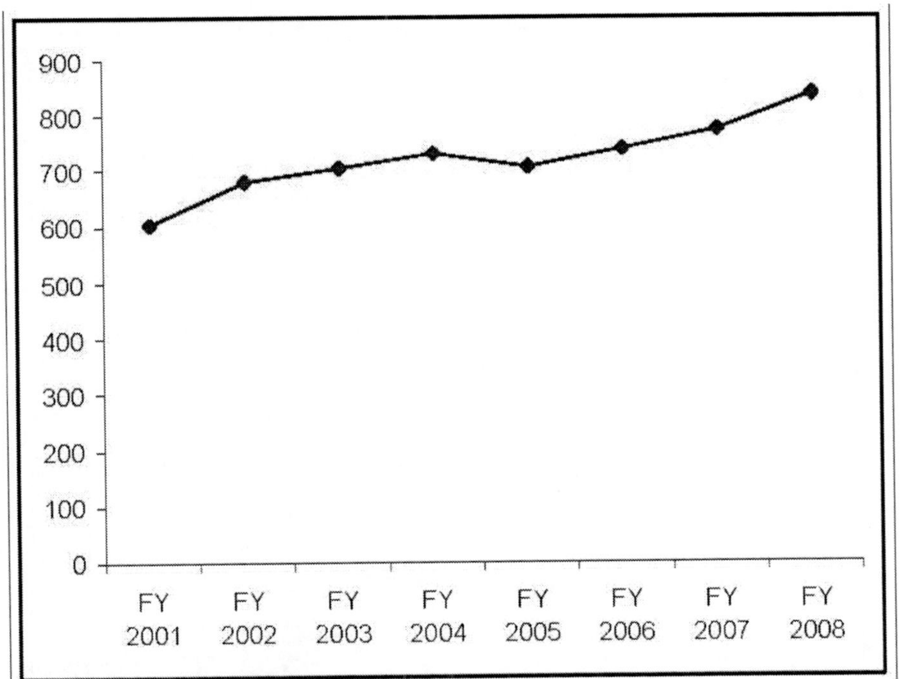

Source: CRS Analysis of Comptroller General annual reports to Congress for FY 2001 – FY 2008.

Figure 8. Number of Bid Protests Filed Against DOD FY2001 – FY2008

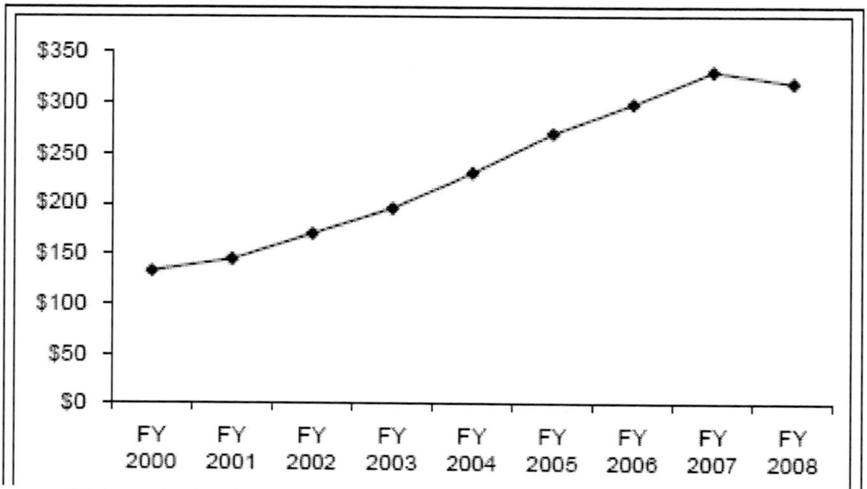

Source: CRS Analysis of Data from USASpending.gov.

Figure 9. DOD Contract Spending FY2001 - FY2008 (in Billions)

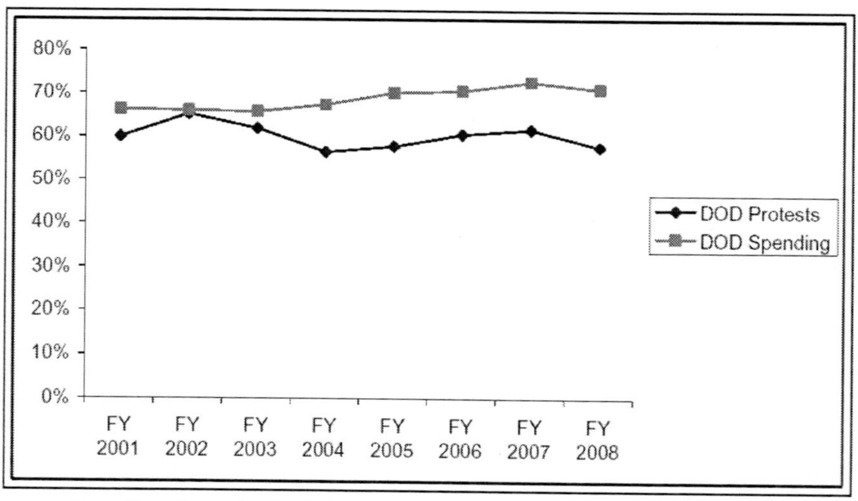

Source: Spending data obtained from USASpending.gov. Protest data obtained from GAO.

Note: Data based on federal contract awards, by funding agency.

Figure 10. DOD Share of All Federal Contract Spending and Bid Protests FY 2001 – FY 2008

Protests against DOD are not sustained at a higher rate than the rest of government (see **Table A-2**). From FY2001 to FY2008, just under 5% of all protests filed against DOD were sustained by GAO, compared to 6% of all protests filed against all federal civilian agencies. During the same period, on average, 60% of all bid protests filed with GAO contested DOD contracts even though DOD accounted for an average of 69% of all federal contract spending (see **Figure 10**).

OPTIONS FOR CONGRESS

In assessing whether legislative action could help minimize the number of protests filed with GAO or the delay of award/execution often associated with a protest being sustained, Congress may consider the options discussed below.

Require agencies re-competing a contract as a result of a GAO opinion to amend or reissue the request for proposal within a specified timeframe of publish why the timeframe can not be met.

According to many analysts, the most significant delays in contract award/execution occur when agencies re-compete an award as a result of a GAO opinion. Requiring agencies to amend of reissue a request for proposal within a specified timeframe—or publish why they are unable to meet the requirement—could encourage agencies to re-compete contracts more quickly.

Requier GAO to include in its annual report to Congress the most common grounds for sustaining protests.

GAO is required to submit to Congress an annual report on bid protests. The report, which is publicly available, includes the number of bid protests filed and instances where agencies did not implement GAO's recommendations. Including in the report the most common reasons bid protests are sustained could help all agencies identify those aspects of contracting that need to be improved. Such improvements could help reduce the number of protests being filed and sustained. Such a report could also help Congress get a better understanding of the weaknesses in the federal acquisition process and consider any legislative action they deem appropriate.

APPENDIX A. BID PROTESTS FILED AGAINST DOD

Table A-1. Bid Protests Filed against DOD

	Total Cases	Protests Sustained	Percent sustained	Total Cases	Protests Sustained	Percent sustained
	Air Force			Army		
FY 2001	145	5	3%	224	12	5%
FY 2002	136	4	3%	254	11	4%
FY 2003	154	2	1%	229	20	9%
FY 2004	132	3	2%	324	18	6%
FY 2005	127	13	10%	282	7	2%
FY 2006	148	13	9%	334	12	4%
FY 2007	136	16	12%	323	22	7%
FY 2008	154	9	6%	396	9	2%
Average	142	8	6%	296	14	5%
	Marines			Navy		
FY 2001	25	6	24%	116	7	6%
FY 2002	16	-	0%	120	5	4%
FY 2003	20	-	0%	148	1	1%
FY 2004	14	3	21%	112	11	10%
FY 2005	12	1	8%	135	5	4%
FY 2006	32	1	3%	101	4	4%
FY 2007	20	-	0%	129	8	6%
FY 2008	22	2	9%	126	9	7%
Average	20	2	8%	123	6	5%
	DLA			DOD(Misc)		
FY 2001	80	3	4%	13	7	54%
FY 2002	119	0	0%	35	2	6%
FY 2003	107	1	1%	46	8	17%
FY 2004	115	1	1%	34	0	0%
FY 2005	121	0	0%	29	2	7%
FY 2006	70	3	4%	54	5	9%
FY 2007	97	0	0%	70	16	23%
FY 2008	87	1	1%	53	0	0%
Average	100	1	1%	42	5	14%

Source: CRS analysis of data provided by GAO.

Notes: Data is based on cases closed and does not include requests for reconsideration; therefore data may not reconcile with information contained in GAO's annual report to Congress.

Table A-2. Comparison of Protests Filed against DOD vs. Civilian Agencies

	Civilian		DOD		Civilian + DOD					
	Total Cases	Decisions Sustained	Total Cases	Decisions Sustained	Total Cases	Total Sustained	Percent Sustained Civilian	Percent Sustained DOD	% Cases from DOD	% Sustain from DOD
FY 2001	404	26	603	40	1,007	66	6%	7%	60%	61%
FY 2002	365	19	680	22	1,032	41	5%	3%	65%	54%
FY 2003	435	18	704	32	1,139	50	4%	5%	62%	64%
FY 2004	565	39	731	36	1,296	75	7%	5%	56%	48%
FY 2005	517	43	706	28	1,223	71	8%	4%	58%	39%
FY 2006	483	34	739	38	1,222	72	7%	5%	60%	53%
FY 2007	483	27	775	62	1,258	89	6%	8%	62%	70%
FY 2008	616	30	838	30	1,454	60	5%	4%	58%	50%

Source: CRS Analysis of data provided by GAO.

Notes: Data does not include requests for reconsideration and therefore may not reconcile with information contained in GAO's annual report to Congress.

End Notes

[1] Bid protests are formal, written objections to an agency's solicitation for bids or offers; cancelation of a solicitation; or award or proposed award of a contract. See: 31 U.S.C. § 3551(1)(A)-(D).

[2] This figure includes 89 requests for reconsideration and 87 bid protests filed as a result of GAO's expanded jurisdiction over task orders (49 filings), A-76 protests (30 filings), and Transportation Security Administration protests (8 filings). See GAO, *GAO Bid Protest Annual Report to the Congress for Fiscal Year 2008*, Dec. 22, 2008, available at http://www.gao.gov/special.pubs/bidpro08.pdf. Last visited, January 13, 2009.

[3] *See, e.g.*, Dana Hedgepeth & Robert O'Harrow, Jr., Air Force Faulted over Handling of Tanker Deal, *Washington Post*, June 19, 2008, at A1; Michael Fabey, Lockheed Martin Files Another CSAR-X Protest, *Aviation Week*, June 12, 2007, *available at* http://www.aviationweek.com/aw/generic/story.jsp?id=news/CSAR061207.xml&headline=Lockheed%20Martin%20Fi les%20Another%20CSAR-X%20Protest&channel=defense.

[4] *See,* Air Force Aerial Refueling Tanker Replacement: Hearing before the House Committee on Armed Services, July 10, 2008; KC-X Tanker Recompete Act, H.R. 6426, 110th Congress, at § 2(a).

[5] Memorandum for Secretaries of the Military Departments, Chairman of the Joint Chiefs of Staff, Under Secretaries of Defense, Aug. 24, 2007, available at http://acquisition.navy.mil/rda/content/download/5263/23838/file/enhancing%20competition%201-18-2008.pdf.

[6] *Duncan Hunter National Defense Authorization Act for Fiscal Year 2009: Report of the Committee on Armed Services, House of Representatives,* 110th Congress, *on H.R. 5658*, at 394-95 (2008).

[7] For more on GAO generally, see CRS Report RL30349, *GAO: Government Accountability Office and General Accounting Office*, by Frederick M. Kaiser.

[8] See Pub.L. 413 and Pub.L. 152, respectively.

[9] The FAR was established to codify uniform policies for acquisition of supplies and services by executive agencies. It is issued and maintained jointly, by the Secretary of Defense, Administrator of General Services, and the Administrator, National Aeronautics and Space Administration. The official FAR appears in the Code of Federal Regulations at 48 CFR Chapter 1. For more information, see http://acquisition.gov/far/index.html. Last visited January 22, 2009.

[10] For a copy of the FAR, see http://www.arnet.gov/far/. Last visited January 5, 2008.

[11] FAR 1.102.

[12] Ibid.

[13] *History of Government Contracting*, p. 49.

[14] For more information on the federal acquisition process, see CRS Report RS22536, *Overview of the Federal Procurement Process and Resources*, by L. Elaine Halchin

[15] An interested party is "an actual or prospective offeror whose direct economic interest would be affected by the award of a contract or by the failure to award a contract." See FAR 33.101.

[16] A protest is a written objection to a contract award by an interested party. See FAR 33.101.

[17] See Clinger-Cohen Act of 1996, Pub. L. 104-106, 110 Stat. 679 (1996) and Administrative Dispute Resolution Act of 1996, Pub.L. 104-320, 110 Stat. 3870 (1996). See also W. Noel Keyes, *Government Contracts Under the Federal Acquisition Regulation*, 3rd ed. (West Publishing, 2003), p. 734. See 31 U.S.C. § 3556 for the authority of the awarding agency, GAO, and COFC to hear bid protests.

[18] See FAR Subpart 19.3

[19] GAO was established in 1921 as an independent auditor of government agencies and activities by the Budget and Accounting Act of 1921 (42 Stat. 23). Today, GAO provides a variety of

services to Congress that extend beyond its original functions and duties, including oversight, investigation, review, and evaluation of executive programs, operations, and activities. For more information on the GAO, see CRS Report RL30349, *GAO: Government Accountability Office and General Accounting Office*, by Frederick M. Kaiser. See also the GAO website at [http://www.gao.gov].

[20] 31 U.S.C. § 3554(a)(1).

[21] 4 C.F.R. § 21.1(f).

[22] GAO, Office of General Counsel, *Bid Protests at GAO: A Descriptive Guide*, 8th ed. (2006), "Background," ¶1, *available at* http://www.gao.gov/special.pubs/og96024.htm.

[23] 4 C.F.R. § 21.7(a).

[24] 31 U.S.C. § 3554(a)(1). The GAO must also resolve timely supplemental or amended protests within this timeframe, if possible. 4 C.F.R. § 21.9(c).

[25] 31 U.S.C. § 3553(c)-(d). However, in certain circumstances, a timely protests will not result in an automatic stay.

[26] 31 U.S.C. § 3554(b)(1)(A)-(G).

[27] 31 U.S.C. § 3554(b)(3).

[28] *Id.*

[29] Based on CRS Analysis of Comptroller General annual reports to Congress for FY 2001 – FY 2008. See http://www.gao.gov/decisions/bidproan.htm for copies of the reports.

[30] 4 C.F.R. § 21.14(a).

[31] 31 U.S.C. § 3556.

[32] See U.S. Government Accountability Office, *GAO Bid Protest Annual Report to the Congress for Fiscal Year 2008*, December 22, 2008, available at http://www.gao.gov/special.pubs/bidpro08.pdf. Last visited, January 13, 2009.

[33] For more information on GAO's expanded jurisdiction, see *GAO Bid-Protests: An Overview of Its Timeframes and Procedures*.

[34] Ibid.

[35] Some have attributed the increase in the effectiveness rate to the predictable nature of GAO opinions. If GAO decisions are sufficiently predictable to allow agencies to determine how GAO will rule in a given situation, agencies are more likely to voluntarily take corrective action than wait for GAO to sustain a protest.

[36] See Donna Borak, "GAO Says Federal Contract Protests by US Businesses Hit 10-Year High in 2008," *Associated Press Newswires*, December 30, 2008; Robert Brodsky, "Bid Protests Reach 10-Year High," *Nextgov.com*, January 5, 2009, www.nextgov.com.

[37] Contract actions reported by *USASpending.gov* includes contract modifications and other actions that can not be protested to GAO. Because the data set for contract actions is more expansive that the pool of actions that can be protested with GAO, the analyses that follow are used to identify trends.

[38] Data is *USASpending.gov* is updated frequently; data from the website that is used in this chapter was accessed on February 10, 2009. FY2008 data may not be complete. OMB established *USASpending.gov* as required by the Federal Funding Accountability and Transparency Act of 2006 Pub. L. No. 109-282, 120 Stat. 1186 (Sept. 26, 2006), 31 U.S.C. § 6101 note. According to GAO, concerns have been raised over the accuracy of the data contained on the website. Given these reliability concerns, data from USASpending.gov is only used in this chapter to identify broad trends. See http://www.gao.gov/transition_2009/agency/omb/ensuring_awards.php#transition_2009. Last visited January 9. 2009.

[39] Deflators for converting into constant dollars derived from the National Income and Product Accounts Table, Table 1.1.4. Price Indexes for Gross Domestic Product. Last Revised on December 23, 2008. Data not yet available to convert FY2008 data into constant dollars.

[40] Contract actions reported by *USASpending.gov* includes contract modifications and other actions that can not be protested to GAO. Therefore, the data set is more expansive that the pool of actions that can be protested with GAO.

[41] U.S. Government Accountability Office, "GAO Sustains Boeing Bid Protest," press release, June 18, 2008, http://www.gao.gov/press/press-boeing2008jun18_3.pdf.

[42] CICA was enacted as part of the Deficit Reduction Act of 1984, P.L. 98-369, §§ 2701-2753, 98 Stat. 1175 (1984) (codified, in part, at 31 U.S.C. § 3556).

[43] 31 U.S.C. § 3553(c)(1).

[44] 31 U.S.C. § 3553(d)(1).

[45] 31 U.S.C. 3553(c) and (d)

[46] 31 U.S.C. § 3553(c)(1) & (d)(3). See Ameron, Inc. v. U.S. Army Corp. of Eng'rs, 607 F. Supp. 962, 974 (D.N.J. 1985) (describing the override as a "built-in safety value to prevent undue harm" to the government).

[47] See Companion report, GAO Bid-Protests: An Overview of Its Timeframes and Procedures, etal.

[48] See Companion report, GAO Bid-Protests: An Overview of Its Timeframes and Procedures etal.

[49] 31 U.S.C. § 3554(a)(1). The GAO must also resolve timely supplemental or amended protests within this timeframe, if possible. 4 C.F.R. § 21.9(c).

[50] Based on conversation with GAO officials, December 17, 2008. According to officials, even in those cases where a supplemental protest is filed, the supplemental protest is generally resolved within 100 days of the filing of the original bid protest.

[51] 31 U.S.C. § 3554(a)(2); 4 C.F.R. § 21.10.

[52] 4 C.F.R. § 21.10(e).

[53] Donna Borak, "GAO Says Federal Contract Protests by US Businesses Hit 10-Year High in 2008," *Associated Press Newswires*, December 30, 2008

[54] Based on conversation with GAO officials, December 17, 2008.

[55] For a copy of the GAO decision, see http://www.gao.gov/decisions/bidpro/311344.htm.

[56] See 41 U.S.C. 262(b) (written findings), 41 U.S.C. 417 (recording requirements), and FAR Subpart 4.8 (detailed requirements implementing the regulations).

[57] Data provided by GAO.

[58] Deflators for converting into constant dollars derived from Office of the Under Secretary of Defense (Comptroller), Department of Defense, National Defense Budget Estimates for FY2009, Department of Defense Deflators – TOA 'Total Non-Pay', p. 47, March 2009.

[59] CRS was unable to ascertain whether the average dollar value of a contract increased, decreased, or remained constant. Such information would help evaluate more precisely the correlation between the increase in bid protests and the increase in contract spending.

In: Government Awards and Objections: Bid... ISBN: 978-1-61728-680-3
Editor: Matthew A. Sauter

Chapter 3

GAO BID PROTEST: 2009 REPORT TO CONGRESS*

Lynn H. Gibson

B-158766
January 8, 2010

The Honorable Nancy Pelosi
Speaker of the House
of Representatives
Dear Madam Speaker:

This letter responds to the requirement of the Competition in Contracting Act of 1984, 31 U.S.C. § 3554(e)(2) (2006), that the Comptroller General report to Congress each instance in which a federal agency did not fully implement a recommendation made by our Office in connection with a bid protest decided the prior fiscal year. There was one such occurrence in fiscal year 2009, regarding our recommendation in *Mission Critical Solutions*, B-401057, May 4, 2009, 2009 CPD ¶ 93, recon. denied, *Small Business Administration—Recon.*, B-401057.2, July 6, 2009, 2009 CPD ¶148. We reported

* This is an edited, reformatted and augmented version of a U. S. Government Accountability Office publication dated January 2010.

the matter to Congress on October 23, 2009, pursuant to 31 U.S.C. § 3554(e)(1). Enclosed is a copy of that report, as well as copies of our decisions in the case explaining in greater detail the particulars surrounding the procurement.

During the fiscal year, we received 1,898 protests (including 64 cost claims) and 91 requests for reconsideration, for a total of 1,989 cases. We closed 1,920 cases: 1,822 protests (including 60 cost claims), 96 requests for reconsideration, and 2 non-statutory decisions. Enclosed for your information is a chart comparing the bid protest activity for fiscal years 2005-2009.

A copy of this chapter, with the enclosures, is being furnished to the Chairman and Ranking Minority Member of the House Committee on Government Reform. A similar report is being furnished to the President of the Senate.

Suicerely yours,

LytonHH. Gibson Acting General Counsel
Enclosures

Bid Protest Statistics for Fiscal Years 2005-2009

	FY 2009	FY 2008	FY 2007	FY 2006	FY 2005
Cases Filed[1]	1,989[2] (up 20%[3])	1,652 (up 17%)	1,411 (up 6%)	1,326 (down 2%)	1,356 (down 9%)
Cases Closed	1,920	1,582	1,394	1,275	1,341
Merit (Sustain + Deny) Decisions	315	291	335	251	306
Number of Sustains	57	60	91	72	71
Sustain Rate	18%	21%	27%	29%	23%
Effectiveness Rate (reported)[4]	45%	42%	38%	39%	37%
ADR[5] (cases used)	149	78	62	91	103
ADR Success Rate[6]	93%	78%	85%	96%	91%
Hearings[7]	12% (65 cases)	6% (32 cases)	8% (41 cases)	11% (51 cases)	8% (41 cases)

B401057
October 23, 2009
Congressional Committees

Subiect: *Mission Critical Solutions*. B-401057. Mav 4. 2009. 2009 CPD If 93. recon. denied, *Small Business Adminisfration-Recon*., B-401057.2, July 6, 2009, 2009 CPD ¶ 148.

This letter is submitted pursuant to 31 U.S.C. § 3554(e)(1) (2006), which requires our Office to report any case in which a Federal agency fails to implement fully a recommendation of the Comptroller General contained in a bid protest decision. As required by that statute, this chapter includes a comprehensive review of the procurement, including the circumstances surrounding the failure of the contracting agency to implement the recommendation made in the decision, as well as a recommendation for further Congressional action.

The decision in question concerned the Department of the Army's selection of Copper River Information Technology, LLC of Anchorage, Alaska, an 8(a) Alaska Native Corporation, for the award of a sole-source contract for information technology support for the Office of the Judge Advocate General. The protester, Mission Critical Solutions of Tampa, Florida, which is a qualified Historically Underutilized Business Zone (HUBZone) small business, argued that rather than awarding to Copper River on a sole-source basis, the agency should have set the requirement aside for competition among HUBZone small businesses.

Our Office found that it was improper for the agency to proceed with a sole-source award to Copper River without considering whether a set-aside for HUBZone concerns was required. We based our conclusion on the plain language of the HUBZone statute, which provides in relevant part that "notwithstanding any other provision of law," "a contract opportunity shall be awarded pursuant to this section on the basis of competition restricted to qualified HUBZone small business concerns if the contracting officer has a reasonable expectation that not less than 2 qualified HUBZone small business concerns will submit offers and that the award can be made at a fair market price." 15 U.S.C. § 657a. We recommended that the agency undertake reasonable efforts to determine whether two or more qualified HUBZone small business concerns would submit offers and whether award could be made at a reasonable price if the contract opportunity were set aside for competition among HUBZone firms, and that if there were such an expectation, that the requirement be resolicited on the basis of competition restricted to HUBZone small business concerns. We also recommended that the agency reimburse the protester the costs of filing and pursuing its protest, including reasonable attorneys' fees.

By letter dated June 24, 2009, the Department of the Army notified our Office that it would be fully implementing the corrective action that we had recommended. In a subsequent letter dated September 28, 2009, the agency advised us that it had reversed its decision, and that rather than implementing our recommendation, it intended to make an award consistent with its original intent (*i.e.*, as a sole-source award to an 8(a) firm). The agency explained that it was taking this action in response to an August 21, 2009 Memorandum Opinion by the Office of the Deputy Assistant Attorney General, Office of Legal Counsel, Department of Justice, which in effect directed executive branch agencies to follow the Small Business Administration's (SBA) regulations placing the different categories of small businesses on an equal footing for the competition and award of contracts. (The SBA regulations in question, 13 C.F.R. §§ 126.605, 126.606, 126.607, essentially provide that HUBZone set-asides are not required even where the criteria specified in 15 U.S.C. § 657a(b)(2)(B) are satisfied if the requirement has previously been performed by an 8(a) contractor or the contracting officer has chosen to offer the requirement to the 8(a) program.)

The Department of Justice opinion notwithstanding, we continue to read the plain language of the HUBZone statute as requiring an agency to set aside an acquisition for competition restricted to qualified HUBZone small business concerns where it has a reasonable expectation that not less than two qualified HUBZone small business concerns will submit offers and that the award can be made at a fair market price. As we explained in a September 14, 2009 letter to various Congressional Committees, this is strictly a legal determination on the part of our Office and is not intended to express a preference—in one direction or the other—about whether the HUBZone program should have priority over other set-aside programs, or whether there should be parity among the programs; we recognized that the foregoing matter is a question of policy to be resolved by Congress. In our September 14 letter, we stated our belief that the acquisition community would benefit from statutory guidance clarifying whether Congress intends for there to be parity or priority among the various set- aside programs. We continue to believe that such guidance would be helpful and recommend that Congress enact legislation clarifying its intent.

Enclosed for your review are copies of our decision on the protest and our September 14 letter to the Committees, as well as the Department of the Army's letters dated June 24 and September 28.

Sincerely yours,

Lynn H. Gibson
Acting General Counsel

Enclosures

cc: The Honorable Daniel K Inouye
Chairman
The Honorable Thad Cochran
Vice Chairman
Committee on Appropriations
United States Senate

The Honorable Carl Levin
Chairman
The Honorable John McCain
Ranking Member
Committee on Armed Services
United States Senate

The Honorable Joseph I. Lieberman
Chairman
The Honorable Susan M. Collins
Ranking Member
Committee on Homeland Security and Governmental Affairs
United States Senate

The Honorable Mary L. Landrieu
Chair
The *Honorable Olympia J. Snowe*
Ranking Member

Committee on Small Business and Entrepreneurship
United States Senate

The Honorable David R Obey
Chairman
The Honorable Jerry Lewis
Ranking Member
Committee on Appropriations
House of Representatives

The Honorable Ike Skelton
Chairman
The Honorable Howard P. "Buck" McKeon
Ranking Member
Committee on Armed Services
House of Representatives

The Honorable Edolphus Towns
Chairman
The Honorable Darrell Issa
Ranking Member
Committee on Oversight and Government Reform
House of Representatives

The Honorable Nydia M. Velãzquez
Chairwoman
The Honorable Sam Graves
Ranking Member
Committee on Small Business
House of Representatives

DECISION

Matter of: Mission Critical Solutions

File: B-401057

Date: May 4, 2009

John R. Tolle, Esq., and Bryan R. King, Esq., Barton Baker Thomas & Tolle, LLP, for the protester.

Capt. Charles D. Halverson, Department of the Army, and John W. Klein, Esq., and Laura Mann Eyester, Esq., Small Business Administration, for the agencies. Jennifer D. Westfall-McGrail, Esq., and Christine S. Melody, Esq., Office of the General Counsel, GAO, participated in the preparation of the decision.

Digest

Protest is sustained where contracting agency did not consider whether two or more qualified Historically Underutilized Business Zone (HUBZone) small businesses could be expected to submit offers and whether award could be made at a fair market price, as required by the HUBZone statute, 15 U.S.C. § 657a, prior to deciding to award contract to an Alaska Native Corporation on a sole-source basis.

Decision

Mission Critical Solutions (MCS) of Tampa, Florida, a firm that is both an 8(a) program participant and a qualified Historically Underutilized Business Zone (HUBZone) small business, protests the Department of the Army's award of a sole-source contract for information technology (IT) support for the Office of the Judge Advocate General to Copper River Information Technology, LLC, of Anchorage, Alaska, an Alaska Native Corporation. The protester argues that rather than awarding to Copper River on a sole-source basis, the agency should have competed the requirement among HUBZone small businesses.

We sustain the protest.

Background

The agency reports that prior to January 2008, the IT support services at issue here were provided by a large business. In December 2007, the Army notified the Small Business Administration (SBA) that the effort was appropriate for set-aside under SBA's 8(a) program and that it intended to award a sole-source contract to MCS (the protester). SBA accepted the requirement into the 8(a) program and authorized the Army to negotiate directly with MCS. On January 31, 2008, the Army awarded MCS a 1-year contract for approximately $3.45 million.

Near the conclusion of the 1-year period of performance, the Army determined that it would structure the follow-on contract for the services to include a base and 2 option years. Because this raised the anticipated value of the contract to an amount in excess of $3.5 million, a sole-source award to the incumbent contractor was precluded by Federal Acquisition Regulation (FAR) § 19.805-1; as relevant here, that provision states that, unless SBA accepts the requirement on behalf of a concern owned by an Indian tribe or an Alaska Native Corporation, an acquisition offered to SBA under the 8(a) program must be awarded on the basis of competition limited to eligible 8(a) firms if (1) there is a reasonable expectation that at least two eligible and responsible 8(a) firms will submit offers and that award can be made at a fair market price, and (2) the anticipated total value of the contract, including options, will exceed $3.5 million (for non-manufacturing acquisitions). The Army then determined that an 8(a) Alaska Native Corporation firm, Copper River Information Technology, LLC, was capable of performing the requirement. On December 17, 2008, the Army notified SBA that, if SBA concurred, it intended to award a contract to Copper River. On December 23, SBA accepted the requirement on behalf of Copper River. The Army awarded a contract to Copper River on January 13, 2009. The protester learned of the award on January 22 and protested to our Office on January 29.

Discussion

The protester challenges the agency's decision to make award on a sole-source basis to Copper River, arguing that the HUBZone statute, 15 U.S.C. § 657a (2006), requires that the procurement be set aside for competition among HUBZone small businesses.[8] As explained below, we conclude that it was improper for the agency to proceed with a sole-source award to Copper River without considering whether a set-aside for HUBZone concerns was required.

The HUBZone Program was established by Title VI of the Small Business Reauthorization Act of 1997, Pub. L. No. 105-135, to provide federal contracting assistance to qualified small business concerns located in historically underutilized business zones in an effort to increase employment opportunities, investment, and economic development in those areas. See FAR § 19.1301(b). Section 602(b)(1)(B) of the Act, 15 U.S.C. § 657a, provides that, "notwithstanding any other provision of law," "a contract opportunity *shall* be awarded pursuant to this section on the basis of competition restricted to qualified HUBZone small business concerns if the contracting officer has a reasonable expectation that not less than 2 qualified HUBZone small business concerns will submit offers and that the award can be made at a fair market price.[9] (Emphasis added.) We have interpreted this language to mean that a HUBZone set-aside is mandatory where the enumerated conditions are met. *International Program Group. Inc.*, B-400278, B-400308, Sept. 19, 2008, 2008 CPD **(11** 172 at —.

The statutory language authorizing the 8(a) program differs from the language authorizing the HUBZone program in that it gives the contracting agency the discretion to decide whether to offer a contracting opportunity to SBA for the 8(a) program. In this connection, the statute provides in relevant part as follows:

> In any, case in which [SBA] certifies to any officer of the Government having procurement powers that [SBA] is competent and responsible to perform any specific Government procurement contract to be let by any such officer, such officer shall be authorized in his discretion to let such procurement contract to [SBA] upon such terms and conditions as may be agreed upon between [SBA] and the procurement officer.

15 U.S.C. § 637(a)(1)(A) (2006).

In a case regarding the HUBZone program, the Ninth Circuit distinguished the mandatory language of the HUBZone statute from the discretionary language of the 8(a) statute as follows:

> [A]s the district court noted, "Congress has used the term 'shall' to mandate that certain contracting opportunities be set aside for competition restricted to HUBZone small businesses. With regard to the 8(a) program ... Congress has ... le[ft] to agency discretion the initial offer and acceptance of contracts into the 8(a) Program." [Citation omitted.] The text of the Section 8(a) Program is materially different from that of the HUBZone Program. Accordingly, the discretionary nature of the Section 8(a) Program cannot be imported into the HUBZone Program thereby eliminating the mandatory aspect of the HUBZone Program.

Contract Mgmt. Indus. Inc. v. Rumsfeld, 434 F.3d 1145, 1149 (9th Cir. 2006).[9] Similarly, our Office concluded in *International Program Group, Inc., supra,* that the discretion granted a contracting officer under a program that permits, but does not require, the setting aside of an acquisition for a particular subgroup of small businesses (in that case, the service-disabled veteran-owned (SDVO) small business program) does not supersede the mandatory nature of the HUBZone set-aside program.[10] In view of the mandatory nature of the language in the HUBZone statute, and the discretionary nature of the statutory language authorizing the 8(a) program, we conclude that it was improper for the agency to proceed with a sole-source award to Copper River without considering whether a set-aside for HUBZone concerns was required.[11]

We recognize that our conclusion that an agency must make reasonable efforts to determine whether it will receive offers from two or more HUBZone small businesses, and if so, set the acquisition aside for HUBZone firms, even where a prior contract for the requirement has previously been performed by an 8(a) contractor, is inconsistent with the views of SBA, as argued in connection with this protest and as implemented through its regulations. Those regulations essentially provide that HUBZone set-asides are not required even where the criteria specified in 15 U.S.C. § 657a(b)(2)(B) are satisfied if the requirement has previously been performed by an 8(a) contractor or the contracting officer has chosen to offer the requirement to the 8(a) program. *See* 13 C.F.R. §§ 126.605, 126.606, and 126.607. While an agency's interpretation of a statute that it is responsible for implementing is entitled to substantial deference, and, if reasonable, should be upheld, *Blue Rock Structures,* Inc., B-293134, Feb. 6, 2004, 2004 CPD ¶ 63 at 8, an interpretation that is unreasonable is not entitled to deference. We do not think that SBA's regulatory implementation of the HUBZone and 8(a) statutes is reasonable since it fails to give effect to the mandatory language of the HUBZone statute.[12] We note in this connection that we have reviewed the legislative history pertaining to the HUBZone program and are aware that there has been considerable discussion (expressing differing viewpoints) as to the intended relationship between the 8(a) and HUBZone programs. As we pointed out in *International Program Group, Inc., supra,* however, the starting point of any analysis of the meaning of a statutory provision is the statutory language, and where the language is clear on its face, as the language of the HUBZone statute is here, its plain meaning will be given effect.[13]

Contrary to the position taken by SBA in its comments on the protest, the contracting agency concedes that "before it recommends a requirement for

SBA consideration as a candidate eligible for the 8(a) Program, it must first follow the HUBZone set-aside prescriptive set out in 15 U.S.C. § 657a(b)(2)," Agency Report at 7; that is, it must make reasonable efforts to ascertain whether it will receive offers from at least two HUBZone small business concerns. See *International Program Group, Inc., supra, at 7; Global Solutions Network, Inc.,* B-292568, Oct. 3, 2003, 2003 CPD 174 at 3. The Army asserts, however, that the point at which it was required to investigate whether HUBZone firms could be expected to compete was when the requirement was originally offered to SBA under the 8(a) program (*i.e.*, December 2007), and that any objection_by the protester to the agency's failure to investigate therefore should have been raised at that time and is now untimely.

We disagree. The HUBZone statute requires that a "contract opportunity" be awarded on the basis of competition restricted to HUBZone small business concerns when the enumerated conditions are met, and, in our view, a separate "contract opportunity" arises every time an agency prepares to award a new contract. Our view is supported by SBA's regulations, which define a "contract opportunity" as a situation in which "a requirement for a procurement exists." 13 C.F.R. § 126.103. Moreover, the SBA regulations governing the award of 8(a) contracts clearly anticipate a reevaluation of the potential for competition, and a decision whether the requirement should continue under the 8(a) program, every time the award of a follow-on contract is contemplated. See 13 C.F.R. § 124.503(0).[14] Accordingly, given that MCS protested to our Office within 10 days after learning that the contract opportunity at issue here had been awarded to Copper River, we think that its protest is timely.

In sum, because the Army did not consider whether two or more qualified HUBZone small businesses could be expected to submit offers and whether award could be made at a fair market price, as required by the HUBZone statute, prior to deciding to award to Copper River on a sole-source basis, we sustain MCS's protest. We recommend that the agency undertake reasonable efforts to determine whether two or more qualified HUBZone small business concerns will submit offers and whether award can be made at a reasonable price if the contract opportunity is set aside for competition among HUBZone firms. If there is such an expectation, we recommend that the Army terminate the contract awarded to Copper River and resolicit the requirement on the basis of competition restricted to HUBZone small business concerns. We also recommend that the agency reimburse the protester the costs of filing and pursuing its protest, including reasonable attorneys' fees. 4 C.F.R. § 21.8(d)(1) (2008). The protester's certified claim for costs, detailing the time spent and cost incurred, must be submitted to the agency within 60 days after receiving this decision.

The protest is sustained.

Daniel I. Gordon Acting General Counsel

Decision

Matter of: Small Busiriess Administration—Reconsideration

File: B-401057.2

Date: July 6, 2009

John R. Tolle, Esq., and Bryan R. King, Esq., Barton Baker Thomas & Tolle, LLP, for the protester.

John W. Klein, Esq., and Laura Mann Eyester, Esq., Small Business Administration, for the agency/requester.

Jonathan L. Kang, Esq., and Ralph **0.** White, Esq., Office of the General Counsel, GAO, participated in the preparation of the decision.

Digest

1. Request for reconsideration from the Small Business Administration (SBA), arguing that our Office exceeded its statutory grant of authority to decide bid protests when we concluded in *Mission Critical Solutions,* B-401057, May 4, 2009, 2009 CPD ¶ 93, that set-asides under the Historically Underutilized Business Zone (HUBZone) program are mandatory where the enumerated conditions of the HUBZone statute are met, is denied where, despite the SBA's contentions to the contrary, our decision did not "invalidate" the SBA's conflicting regulation, and the decision, and the recommendation within it, were consistent with our statutory jurisdiction.
2. Request for reconsideration of prior decision sustaining protest is denied where newly raised information fails to show that our prior decision contains any errors of fact or law.

Decision

The Small Business Administration (SBA) asks that we reconsider our decision in *Mission Critical Solutions,* B-401057, May 4, 2009, 2009 CPD ¶ 93, in which we concluded that, prior to the award of a contract to an Alaska Native Corporation on a sole-source basis, the statute authorizing a preference for Historically Underutilized Business Zone (HUBZone) small businesses requires a contracting agency to first consider whether two or more qualified HUBZone small businesses could be expected to submit offers and whether award could be made at a fair price. The SBA argues that our decision erred in concluding that the HUBZone statute creates a mandatory preference for HUBZone small businesses over the preference for 8(a) businesses.

We deny the request for reconsideration.

Background

Our decision in *Mission Critical Solutions, supra,* addressed the statutory requirements for the HUBZone and 8(a) programs, and the SBA regulations that implement these programs. The HUBZone Program was established by Title VI of the Small Business Reauthorization Act of 1997, Pub. L. No. 105-135, to provide federal contracting assistance to qualified small business concerns located in historically underutilized business zones in an effort to increase employment opportunities, investment, and economic development in those areas. See Federal Acquisition Regulation (FAR) § 19.1301(b). Section 602(b)(1)(B) of the Act provides as follows:

> [N]otwithstanding any other provision of law . . . a contract opportunity *shall* be awarded pursuant to this section on the basis of competition restricted to qualified HUBZone small business concerns if the contracting officer has a reasonable expectation that not less than 2 qualified HUBZone small business concerns will submit offers and that the award can be made at a fair market price.

15 U.S.C. § 657a (emphasis added).

Based on the statute's use of the phrase "shall be awarded," we have interpreted this language to mean that a HUBZone set-aside is mandatory where the enumerated conditions are met. *International Program Group. Inc.,* B-400278, B-400308, Sept. 19, 2008, 2008 CPD 172 at 5.

The statutory language authorizing the 8(a) program differs from the language authorizing the HUBZone program in that it gives the contracting agency the discretion to decide whether to offer a contracting opportunity to the SBA for the 8(a) program. In this connection, the statute provides:

> In any case in which [SBA] certifies to any officer of the Government having procurement powers that [SBA] is competent and responsible to perform any specific Government procurement contract to be let by any such officer, such officer shall be authorized in his discretion to let such procurement contract to [SBA] upon such terms and conditions as may be agreed upon between [SBA] and the procurement officer.

15 U.S.C. § 637(a)(1)(A) (2006).

MCS—a participant in the SBA's 8(a) program and a qualified HUBZone small business—challenged the award of a sole-source contract by the Department of the Army for information technology (IT) support for the Office of the Judge Advocate General to Copper River Information Technology, LLC, an Alaska Native Corporation. The requirements had been previously performed by MCS under an 8(a) set-aside.[15]

In our decision, dated May 4, 2009, we agreed with the protester's contention that the Army should have competed the requirement among HUBZone small businesses, rather than awarding to Copper River on a sole-source basis. Specifically, we concluded that, in view of the mandatory nature of the language in the HUBZone statute, and the discretionary nature of the statutory language authorizing the 8(a) program, an agency must first consider whether a set-aside for HUBZone small business concerns is required, before making a sole-source award to an 8(a) or Alaska Native Corporation. *Mission Critical Solutions, supra,* at 4-5. Our decision recognized that our conclusion regarding the HUBZone statute was inconsistent with the SBA's regulations, which state that

> a contracting activity may not make a requirement available for a HUBZone contract if: . . . [a]n 8(a) participant currently is performing the requirement through the 8(a)BD [business development] program or the SBA has accepted the requirement for award through the 8(a)BD program, unless the SBA has consented to release the requirement from the 8(a)BD program.

13 C.F.R. § 126.605.

On May 14, the SBA requested that we reconsider our decision.

Discussion

Our Bid Protest Regulations require that a party requesting reconsideration "must show that our prior decision contains errors of either fact or law, or must present information not previously considered that warrants reversal or modification of our decision." 4 C.F.R. § 21.14(a) (2009). Our Office will not consider "a request for reconsideration based on repetition of arguments previously raised." *Id.*

The SBA's request for reconsideration primarily states its disagreement with our legal analysis regarding the statutory requirements for HUBZone set-asides.[16] Much of the agency's request addresses matters that were raised during the protest and discussed in our decision; those issues need not be addressed again.

We discuss below, however, the following three arguments raised by the SBA: (1) that the decision overstepped the statutory authority granted to the Government Accountability Office (GAO) to decide bid protests by "invalidating," in the SBA's view, a regulation properly promulgated by the executive branch agency charged with administering and interpreting the Small Business Act; (2) that the decision erred, as a matter of law, in its interpretation of the phrase "notwithstanding any other provision of law" found in the HUBZone statute; and (3) that the decision incorrectly stated the trial and appellate court holdings in *Contract Management Inc. v. Rumsfeld,* (291 F. Supp. 2d 1166 (D. Hawaii 2003), and 434 F.3d 1145 (9th Cir. 2006), respectively), which discussed the statutory provisions for the HUBZone and 8(a) programs. As set forth more fully below, we think none of these contentions provides a basis to grant this request for reconsideration.

GAO's Statutory Authority to Decide Bid Protests

First, the SBA argues that our decision improperly concluded that its regulations concerning HUBZone set-asides are inconsistent with the HUBZone statute because lilt is not within GAO's authority to decide whether an agency's regulation is reasonable and void an agency's regulations." Request for Reconsideration at 5. We think that the SBA mischaracterizes the holding of our decision, and that the decision was consistent with our statutory authority.

The jurisdiction of our Office to hear bid protests is established by the Competition in Contracting Act of 1984 (CICA), 31 U.S.C. §§ 3551-3556

(2006). Under CICA, our Office has the authority to "determine whether [a] solicitation, proposed award, or award complies with statute and regulation." 31 U.S.C. § 3554(b)(1). As the SBA notes, bid protest decisions by our Office—an independent, nonpartisan, legislative branch agency—are not binding on executive branch agencies. See *Bowsher v. Synar,* 478 U.S. 714, 727-32.

Instead, our authorizing statute requires that if we conclude that an agency action violates a procurement law or regulation, we "shall recommend that the Federal agency" take actions such as "terminat[ing] the contract," or "award[ing] a contract consistent with the requirements of such statute and regulation." 31 U.S.C. § 3554(c). Upon receipt of such a recommendation from our Office, the executive branch agency is required to advise the Comptroller General by letter if the agency does not implement our recommendation. Id. The Comptroller General is required to report to the cognizant congressional committees each instance in which a federal agency did not implement our recommendation. 31 U.S.C. § 3554(e).

Our decision held that the plain meaning of the HUBZone statute creates a mandatory preference for HUBZone small business concerns when the enumerated conditions of the statute are met. *Mission Critical Solutions, supra*, at 7. Both the district court and the appellate court decisions cited by the SBA, and discussed in detail below, reached precisely the same conclusion. 291 F. Supp. 2d at 1166; 434 F.3d at 1149.

With respect to the SBA's concerns about its regulation, we acknowledged in our decision that our conclusions regarding the HUBZone statute were "inconsistent with the views of the SBA, as argued in connection with this protest and as implemented through its regulations," specifically, 13 C.F.R. §§ 126.605, 126.606, and 126.607. *Id.* at 5. Nonetheless, as we also explained, while an agency's interpretation of a statute it is responsible for implementing is entitled to substantial deference— and, if reasonable, should be upheld—an agency interpretation that is unreasonable is not entitled to deference. Id. (citing *Blue Rock Structures, Inc.,* B-293134, Feb. 6, 2004, 2004 CPD ¶ 63 at 8). In sum, we conclude that our decision, and the recommendation within it, were consistent with our statutory jurisdiction.

Effect of "Notwithstanding" Language on Other Small Business Programs

Next, the SBA provides new information regarding its argument that the phrase in the HUBZone statute, "notwithstanding any other provision of law," should not be interpreted literally. During the course of the underlying protest, the SBA argued that this phrase should not be given its literal meaning because to do so would conflict with—and by implication repeal, in the SBA's view—the goals set under the Small Business Act for contracting with various categories of small businesses. See 15 U.S.C. § 644(g)(1). Specifically, the SBA contends that our decision would require contracting agencies to give priority to HUBZone small business concerns for all small business set-asides, and would hinder contracting agencies' ability to meet their goals for contracting with other types of small businesses, such as 8(a) firms.

We addressed this argument in our decision, noting that the SBA had not provided information to support its position. *Mission Critical Support, supra*, at 6 n.7. Further, we noted that the SBA's argument ignores the plain language of the HUBZone statute, which distinguishes that program from others, such as the 8(a) program, which have non-mandatory set-aside requirements. Id.

In its request for reconsideration, the SBA provided data which show that there are more registered HUBZone small business concerns than 8(a) participants for the construction and computer services industries.[18] Request for Reconsideration at 14. The agency again contends that our decision will prevent executive branch agencies from meeting their contracting goals, because all requirements will be awarded to HUBZone small business concerns, instead of the other contractors.

We think the SBA's data about the numbers of different types of HUBZone and 8(a) businesses do not establish that respecting the plain language of the HUBZone statute will effectively "repeal" the Small Business Act's contracting goals. In any event, even if that impact were established, we would not see a basis to interpret the "notwithstanding" language in a way that does not give effect to its plain meaning.[19]

The *Contract Management* Decisions

Finally, the SBA contends that our decision misinterpreted the holdings of the two *Contract Management* decisions. Specifically, the SBA argues that the district court agreed with the agency's view "that HUBZone set-asides are not mandatory in every case and the court did not rule that HUBZone set asides take priority over the 8(a) [business development] or [the service-disabled veteran-owned small business concern] programs." Request for Reconsideration at 15. We stand by our view that these decisions support our conclusion that a HUBZone set aside is mandatory where the statute's enumerated conditions are met. See *Mission Critical Solutions, supra,* at 6 n.6, 7.

As a preliminary matter, the SBA seems to overlook the fact that the two *Contract Management* decisions addressed a challenge to an agency's decision to set aside a procurement for HUBZone small business concerns, rather than small business concerns, and the fact that, in both cases the courts rejected the argument that the HUBZone program should be viewed as providing for discretionary set-asides for small businesses, similar to the 8(a) program. In addition, both courts expressly concluded that the statutory language concerning the HUBZone program was mandatory, and therefore took precedence over a small business set-aside. In so doing, both courts distinguished between the HUBZone program's mandatory language, and the 8(a) program's discretionary language. 291 F. Supp. 2d at 1176; 434 F.3d at 1149.

Despite the underlying holdings of these decisions, the SBA correctly observes that the district court also stated that the SBA's regulations "sufficiently promote the congressional objective of parity between the HUBZone and 8(a) programs." 291 F. Supp. 2d at 1176-77. The SBA argues that our decision ignored the court's conclusion that its regulations were reasonable implementations of congressional intent that the two programs be given parity.

In our view, the district court's discussion of the SBA's regulations concerning the 8(a) program—as distinct from the statutes governing the HUBZone and 8(a) programs—was ancillary to the court's primary holding concerning the mandatory requirements of the HUBZone statute.[20] As mentioned above, however, both the appellate court and district court ultimately concluded, in no uncertain terms, that the HUBZone statute mandates a set-aside, while the statutory language authorizing the 8(a) program is discretionary. 434 F.3d at 1148-49; 291 F. Supp. 2d at 1176. Accordingly, we think our decision is consistent with both of the *Contract Management* decisions. To the extent the SBA continues to argue that our decision was in error, we find no basis to reconsider our decision.

The request for reconsideration is denied.

Daniel I. Gordon

Acting General Counsel

End Notes

[1] All entries in this chart are counted in terms of the docket numbers ("B" numbers) assigned by our Office, not the number of procurements challenged. Where a protester files a supplemental protest or multiple parties protest the same procurement action, multiple iterations ofthe same "B" number are assigned (ie., .2, .3). Each ofthese numbers is deemed a separate protest for purposes of this chart.

[2] Of the 1,989 cases filed m FY 2009,168 are attributable to GAO's recently expanded bid protest jurisdiction over task orders (139filings),A-?6 protests (16 filings), and Transportation Security Administration protests (13 filings). These 168 filings represent 50% of the total increase in filings from FY 2008 to FY 2009 (33? filings).

[3] From the prior fiscal year.

[4] Based on a protester obtaining some form of relief from the agency, as reported to GAO.

[5] Altemative Dispute Resolution.

[6] Percentage resolved without a formal GAO decision.

[7] Percentage of fully developed decisions in which GAO conducted a hearing.

[8] In its initial protest, MCS also asserted that there are firms capable of perfonning the IT services that are both 8(a) program participants and qualified HUBZone small businesses and that the agency was required to compete the requfrement among 8(a) firms that are also HUBZone-certffied, rather than award a confract to Copper River on a sole-source basis. In support ofits position, MCS cited FAR § 19.800(e), which provides tn relevant part that "[iff [an] acquisition is offered to the SBA, SBA regulations (13 C.F.R. § 126.607(b)) give first priority to HUBZone 8(a) concems." SBA (which we invited to comment on the protest) pointed out that the SBA regulation cited in FAR § 19.800(e) as requiring that first priority be given to HUBZone 8(a) concems is no longer hi effect. That is, 13 C.F.R. § 126.607(b) was revised in 2005 to elimuiate the language providing for first priority to HUBZone 8(a) concems. The Civilian Agency Acquisition CouncU and the Defense Acquisition Regulations Council have twice issued proposed rules providing for the amendment of FAR § 19.800(e) to delete the reference to 13 C.F.R. § 126.607(b). 73 Fed. Reg. 12,700, Mar. 10, 2008; 74 Fed. Reg. 16,826, Apr. 13, 2009. The protester has not rebutted the SBA position or made any further argument regarding the appUcability of FAR § 19.800(e); accordingly, we consider it to have abandoned its argument that the agency was requfred to set aside the procurement for HUBZone 8(a) firms.

[9] The statute also provides that a confracting officer "may" award a sole-source confract to a qualffied HUBZone small bushiess concem ff the qualffied HUBZone firm is detennined to be a responsible confractor wdth respect to performance of the contract, and the confracting officer does not have a reasonable expectation that two or more qualffied HUBZone firms wdU submit offers; the anticipated award price of the contract (includmg options) wdU not exceed $5 milUon (in the case of a contract opportunity assigned a standard industrial classification code for manufacturing) or $3 million (in the case of all other confract opportunities); and, ui the estimation of the contracting officer, the confract award can be made at a fafr and reasonable price. 15 U.S.C. § 657a(b)(2)(A).

[10] This decision (and the underlying District Court decision discussed in footnote 6, infra) concemed a chaUenge to an agency's decision to set aside a procurement for HUBZone smaU business concems rather than small businesses.

[11] In its comments on the protest here, SBA argued that "the confracting officer has discretion not necessarily in using the 8(a) prograin, since that is an initial determination made by the SBA, but in deciding whether the 8(a) participant to be UtUized by the SBA is capable of perfonning," and that "[t]he ultimate discretion as to whether a requfrement should be placed in the 8(a) program rests wdth the Adminisfrator ofthe SBA[;] [t]he Administrator will place a requfrement into the 8(a) program when he or she decides it is necessary or appropriate." SBA Comments, Mar. 3, 2009, at 10. We understand SBA to be arguing that

the cited excerpt from 15 U.S.C. § 637(a)(1)(A) does not give the confracting officer the discretion to decUne to place in the 8(a) program a confract that SBA has detennined appropriate for performance under the program, and that the only discretion conferred upon the contracting agency by the 8(a) statute is the discretion to reject SBA's nomination of a specffic contractor for performance. We do not agree with SBA that the only discretion confened upon the contracting agency by the 8(a) statute is the discretion to reject SBA's nomination of a particular confractor for performance. In fact, this constmction of the statute is at odds with SBA's own regulations, which give SBA the right to appeal to the head of the procuring agency-implying that the ultimate authority rests wdth the latter official-" [a] contracting officer's decision not to make a particular procurement available for award as an 8(a) confract." 13 C.F.R. § 124.505(a)(1). Moreover, even assuming that the ultimate discretion as to whether a requfrement should be placed in the 8(a) program rests with the Administrator of SBA, that does not mean that the SBA's discretionaiy authority under the 8(a) statute supersedes the mandatory aspect of the HUBZone program.

[12] In further support ofthis conclusion, 15 U.S.C. § 657a(b)(4) provides that "[a] procurement may not be made from a source on the basis of a preference provided in paragraph (2) or (3), if the procurement would otherwdse be made from a different source under section 4124 or 4125 of titie 18 [acquisitions from Federal Prison Industries] or the Javits-Wagner-O'Day Act (41 U.S.C 46 et seo.)." We view the omission of acquisitions in or offered to the 8(a) program from the contracting preferences expUcitiy exempt from appUcation of the HUBZone statute as further evidence that (Congress did not uitend to exempt these acquisitions from the language making HUBZone set-asides mandatory when the specffied conditions are met.

[13] SBA argues that the district court in *Contract Mgmt. Indus.. Inc. v. Rumsfeld, supra*, "sanctioned" its regulations exempting contract opportunities for requirements that have previously been accepted into the 8(a) program from application of the HUBZone statute. WhUe the court there observed that the SBA regulations were consistent wdth a goal of preventing a conflict between the HUBZone and 8(a) programs, the court did not address the issue before us-whether it was consistent with the mandatory nature of the HUBZone statute for the regulations to exempt certain 8(a) acquisitions from the statute's application.

[14] SBA also argued that the phrase "notwdthstanding any other provision of law" in the HUBZone statute is best interpreted as requiring the disregard only of provisions outside the Small Business Act and not provisions of law contained in the Act, such as those regarding the 8(a) prograin. SBA maintains that this interpretation is consistent wdth other provisions of the Act, including the section setting goals for small business contracting wdth various categories of small businesses, 15 U.S.C. § 644(g)(1). SBA argues that in order for any agency to assist in meeting goals for smaU business confracting, "the agency must be afforded some discretion hi detennining which smaU business program to utiUze." SBA Comments at 10.

SBA appears to be arguing that achievement of the goals set forth in 15 U.S.C. § 644(g)(1) takes precedence over the requirement for HUBZone set-asides. As a preliminary matter, SBA has furnished no evidence to support its position that the setting aside of acquisitions for HUBZone small business concems where the specffied criteria are met wdll prevent the govemment from meeting its goals for confracting wdth other categories of small businesses. Moreover, as pointed out by the district court in *Contract Mgmt. Indus.. Inc. v. Rumsfeld*. 291 F. Supp. 2d 1166 (D. Haw. 2003), "[i]f the HUBZone Program becomes so successful that it threatens the ability of other small businesses to meet their goals. Congress is free to amend the statute." Id at 1176. In any event, while this argument likely reflects SBA's view of the better policy in this area, it does not take into account the plain language ofthe HUBZone statute.

[15] In relevant part, this provision, entitied "Repetitive Acquisitions," states as follows:

A procuring activity contracting officer must submit anew offering letter to SBA where he or she intends to award a follow-on or repetitive contract as an 8(a) award. This enables SBA to detennine:
(1) Whether the requfrement should be a competitive 8(a) award;
(4) Whether the requirement should continue under the 8(a) [business development] program.

16 As discussed in our prior decision, the SBA had accepted the IT support services at issue here into the SBA's 8(a) program and authorized the Army to negotiate dfrectiy wdth MCS. These negotiations led to the award of a 1-year confract to MCS on a sole-source basis. When the agency began its planning for a foUow-on confract, the anticipated value ofthe contract was greater than $3.5 million; thus, the agency decided that a sole-source award to MCS was precluded under FAR § 19.805-1. As relevant here, FAR § 19.805-1 states that-unless the SBA accepts the requfrement on behaff ofa concem owned by an Indian tribe or an Alaska Native Corporation-an acquisition under the 8(a) program must be awarded on the basis of competition limited to eligible 8(a) firms if: (1) there is a reasonable expectation that at least two eligible and responsible 8(a) firms with submit offers, and that award can be made at a fair market price; and (2) the anticipated total value of the confract, including options, will exceed $3.5 milUon (for non-manufacturing acquisitions). The Army then detennined that Copper River, an 8(a) Alaska Native Corporation firm, was capable of performing the requirement, and, wdth the SBA's approval, awarded a sole-source contract to that company.

17 At our Office's invitation, SBA provided its views regarding these matters during the protest.

18 We note that the SBA could have, but did not, provide these data in its comments during the protest.

19 The SBA's request for reconsideration also reiterates its view that three cases cited by the agency during the protest support its view that the phrase "notwdthstanding other provisions of law" should not be apphed Uterally because it would place the mandatory HUBZone requirements in conflict wdth the contracting goals, wdth the effect of repealing the latter. The SBA cites both *Oregon Natural Resources Council v. Thomas*, 92 F.3d 792, 796-97 (9th Cir. 1996) *and In re Glacier Bav Kee Leasing Co*.. 944 F.2d 577, 582 (9th Cir. 1991), which hold generally tiiat repeals of one statutory provision by another must be expressly stated, in support ofits argument that applyuig the plain meaning of the "notwithstanding" provision would result in an improper repeal of the small business contracting goals. We do not find these cases apposite, because, as discussed aboye, we do not agree that tiie data cited by the SBAshow that the HUBZone statute has the effect of repealing these goals, and because, in any event, the plain language of the statute would give explicit priority to the HUBZone program even in the event a confUct between the programs were to arise. The SBA's thfrd case is *E.P. Paup Co. v. Director. Office of Workers Comnensation Programs*. 999 F.2d 1341,1348-49 (9th Cir. 1993), where the court concluded that the phrase "notwdthstanding any other provision oflaw" in a federal statute did not mean that the statute impliedly preempted state law, as such preemptions must be explicitiy set forth. Here, however, there is no issue offederal preemption of state law.

20 For the record, we note that when the district court references a "congressional objective" that there be parity between the HUBZone and 8(a) programs, the court cites the report ofthe Senate Small Business Committee concemuig the Small Busmess Reauthorization Act of 2000 (S. Rep. 106-422 (Sept. 27, 2000)). 291 F. Supp. 2d at 1176. We have found no evidence ofthis "objective" in the statute, which is plain on its face. In confrast, the court of appeals decision did not address this issue. Rather, the court of appeals noted that although this issue had been discussed in the district court decision, it was not raised on appeal. *Contract Management. Inc*.. 434F.3d at 1147n.3.

In: Government Awards and Objections: Bid... ISBN: 978-1-61728-680-3
Editor: Matthew A. Sauter

Chapter 4

REPORT TO CONGRESS ON BID PROTESTS INVOLVING DEFENSE PROCUREMENTS*

United States Government Accountability Office

B-401197
April 9, 2009

The Honorable Carl Levin
Chairman
The Honorable John McCain
Ranking Minority Member
Committee on Armed Services
United States Senate

The Honorable Ike Skelton
Chairman
The Honorable John M. McHugh
Ranking Minority Member
Committee on Armed Services
House of Representatives

---

* This is an edited, reformatted and augmented version of a U. S. Government Accountability Office publication dated April 2009.

Subject: *Report to Congress on Bid Protests Involving Defense Procurements*

This chapter responds to the direction from the Committee on Armed Services, House of Representatives, contained in the report on the Duncan Hunter National Defense Authorization Act for Fiscal Year 2009, Pub. L. No. 110-417 (2008) (H.R. Rep. No. 110-652, at 394-95, May 16, 2008). The committee directed the Comptroller General of the United States to review bid protests filed with the Government Accountability Office (GAO) during the last 5 years associated with procurement actions by the Department of Defense (DOD). The committee requested that we assess the extent to which bid protests may be increasing, the extent to which frivolous and improper protests may be increasing, and the causes of any identified increases. The committee further directed the Comptroller General to provide recommendations regarding actions that Congress, or the executive branch, could take to disincentivize frivolous and improper bid protests on the part of industry.

EXECUTIVE SUMMARY

This chapter reaches the following conclusions about the GAO bid protest process in general, and about the committee's mandate to assess the increase in protests and the extent to which frivolous protests may be increasing:

- Twenty-five years ago, the Competition in Contracting Act of 1984 (CICA), Pub. L. No. 98-369, 98 Stat. 1175 (1984), codified and significantly enhanced GAO's bid protest forum. The existing process provides a balanced approach to adjudicate and resolve challenges to U.S. government procurements.
- Despite an increase in bid protest filings in fiscal year (FY) 2008--driven in part by statutory expansions of GAO's bid protest jurisdiction--the number of protests challenging DOD contract awards in the last 5 years is relatively low when viewed historically.
- The GAO bid protest process significantly reduces potential disruptions to DOD procurements as a result of three factors:
  - GAO consistently closes more than 50 percent of all protests involving DOD procurements within 30 days of filing;
  - The remaining DOD protests must be, and are, resolved within 100 days of filing; and

- CICA permits agencies to proceed with contract performance even before a protest is resolved when the goods or services are urgently needed, or when proceeding is in the best interests of the United States.
- GAO's regulations and procedures currently provide GAO the ability to promptly close protests that do not merit further development. GAO does not need to determine that a protest is "frivolous" to promptly close it, and, in our view, making such a determination could add substantial costs to the protest process and have the unintended consequence of discouraging participation in federal contracting and, in turn, limiting competition.

BACKGROUND

On occasion, bidders or others interested in government procurements may believe that a contract has been, or is about to be, awarded improperly or illegally, or that they have been unfairly denied a contract or an opportunity to compete for a contract. These objections to procurement actions or decisions are referred to as bid protests.

Twenty-five years ago, Congress enacted CICA. In addition to significantly reforming the federal procurement system, CICA provided a statutory basis for the bid protest forum within the Office of General Counsel in GAO.

Last year, a single protested procurement--the Boeing Company's challenge of the award of a contract by the Air Force to Northrop Grumman for a new fleet of tanker planes--generated unprecedented interest in, and questions about, GAO's role in deciding these disputes. While we welcome this interest, many of the questions we received, as well as the media accounts of the dispute, reflected a limited understanding of the protest process.

CICA's 1984 changes to GAO's bid protest forum confirmed and strengthened GAO's long-standing role as a quasi-judicial forum for objective, independent, and impartial resolution of disputes concerning the award of federal contracts. At the heart of the law's bid protest provisions is a balancing act that attempts to ensure that procurements can proceed without undue disruption, while also providing a mechanism for holding agencies accountable, and protecting the rights of aggrieved offerors to fair treatment by the government.

A discussion of the current bid protest process should begin with the concerns expressed by Congress at the time of CICA's enactment. Specifically, the report of the House Committee on Government Operations complained that the GAO bid protest process prior to 1984 was too weak to be effective; was principally advisory in nature; and depended too heavily on voluntary agency compliance--in responding to protests, in producing applicable documents, and in implementing recommended remedies.[1] In fact, the report set forth a detailed example of a protest filed by Amdahl Corporation challenging the award of an Army contract to the IBM Corporation on the basis that the equipment being offered did not comply with the solicitation's requirements, and was out of date and not in current production.[2] Although GAO ultimately sustained the protest,[3] because there was no provision for a stay of performance, the decision was issued after the equipment had been installed, and hence no meaningful relief was available.[4] The window into the procurement process provided by the *Amdahl* protest was the subject of hearings in the House,[5] and led to the above-referenced discussion of the case in the committee report.

To address concerns about the strength of the GAO bid protest forum and the voluntary nature of agency responses to protest allegations, CICA provided a statutory basis for the protest process and set statutory timelines for agency responses. To strike a balance between the need for agencies to proceed with their procurements and the need to allow complaints to be addressed, CICA imposed a deadline on GAO for issuing its decisions. As amended, CICA requires that GAO resolve all bid protests within 100 calendar days; GAO has never failed to meet its statutory deadline for issuing decisions.

Perhaps most significantly, to address concerns about providing meaningful relief when a protest is upheld, CICA included an automatic stay of contract performance until a decision on the protest is issued. CICA's balancing of the competing interests of the government's procurement system is clearly reflected in two provisions addressing this issue of providing meaningful relief. First, the law allows agencies to "override" the automatic stay of performance with a written agency finding that the goods or services are urgently needed, or that proceeding with performance in the face of a protest is in the best interests of the United States. Second, the law requires agencies to advise GAO if the agency decides not to follow the recommendation of a bid protest decision; GAO is then required to report these instances of noncompliance to four congressional committees.[6]

In implementing the bid protest provisions of CICA, GAO has maintained the balance between allowing agency procurements to proceed and providing

meaningful relief to protesters. Before a protest will be considered on the merits, GAO applies a series of tests that, as explained below, screen out a large number of cases. These tests are embodied in GAO's regulations implementing the bid protest provisions of CICA. For example, GAO applies a strict timeliness rule, set out in 4 C.F.R. Part 21, that leads to the prompt dismissal of many protests. In addition, GAO applies a standing rule, based on CICA's definition of an "interested party" with standing to protest. Again, this rule leads to the dismissal of a number of protests. If the protest meets GAO's timeliness and standing rules, GAO reviews it for legal sufficiency. In this regard, our regulations provide other grounds for dismissing protests. When a protest does not state a valid legal basis or raises issues outside GAO's jurisdiction (such as disputes during contract administration and challenges to a firm's size status for purposes of a small-business set-aside), GAO promptly dismisses it.

As discussed in greater detail below, GAO's application of these rules means that a significant percentage of GAO protests are dismissed within a short time after filing, in which case the contracting agency is free to proceed with the procurement (that is, CICA's automatic stay is lifted).

For those cases that GAO does not dismiss, GAO will issue a decision on the merits, always within CICA's 100-day deadline, and typically well before it. In those cases, GAO decides whether the contracting agency complied with the statutes and regulations controlling government procurements. If GAO finds that the agency did not violate procurement law, or that any violation that may have occurred did not prejudice the protester's chances of winning the contract, GAO will deny the protest. If GAO determines that the agency did violate procurement law and the violation prejudiced the protester's chances of winning the contract, GAO will sustain the protest.

GAO's role in resolving a bid protest is an adjudicative process that differs significantly from the audits and evaluations conducted by GAO's audit teams. Protests are handled by a group of 30 attorneys within GAO's Office of General Counsel, who serve as hearing officers. Unlike GAO audit reports, bid protest decisions do not address broad programmatic issues, such as whether a weapons program is being managed effectively and within costs. Nor do our decisions evaluate which company's proposal is better. Rather, the decision produced in response to a protest addresses the specific allegations raised by the parties about whether a particular government action was contrary to procurement law or regulations, or contrary to the evaluation scheme the procuring agency established in the solicitation. Only when GAO finds--after developing a full record--that a procuring agency has not followed procurement rules, and that this failure has prejudiced the protester's chances of winning a competition, do we sustain a protest.

Bid Protest Trends

Summary of Findings

As noted above, we were asked to review the number of GAO protests filed challenging procurement actions by DOD during the last 5 years (FY 2004 to FY 2008) and assess the extent to which protests may be increasing.[7] Based on our review, which shows a historical variability in the number of protest filings, the 4-year period of FY 2004 to 2007 does not reflect an upward trend in DOD protest filings.[8] Rather, as discussed below, the number of protests filed, relative to DOD procurement spending, actually suggests a downward trend in the rate of DOD protest filings.

A single year in this 5-year period, however, FY 2008, did reflect a significant increase in the number of DOD protests filed. Our review indicates that a portion of this increase is tied to recent statutory expansions of GAO's bid protest jurisdiction, and we expect that our expanded jurisdiction will continue to result in an increased level of DOD (and non-DOD) protest filings. One important aspect of our process, however, remained constant--the rate at which DOD protests are closed early in the protest process.

We were also asked to consider the extent to which frivolous protests may be increasing. We limited our inquiry to ascertaining any trends regarding DOD protest filings as a whole, however, because, as discussed more fully in the next section of this chapter, while our Office tracks dismissals and grounds for dismissing protests, we do not label protest filings as frivolous, and accordingly, do not collect data on such filings.

DOD Protests: A Historical Perspective

In order to fully understand and consider the extent to which DOD bid protests may be increasing, we decided to consider the number of protests filed during this period in historical context. Thus, we reviewed not only the number of DOD protests filed during the last 5 years, but also the number of DOD protests, and non-DOD protests, filed over the past 20 years. As can be seen from Figures 1 and 2 below, while the number of DOD protests filed with GAO has fluctuated significantly over the past 20 years (FY 1989 to FY 2008), the last 5 years reflect relatively low numbers of DOD protests filed, in terms of the historical trends.

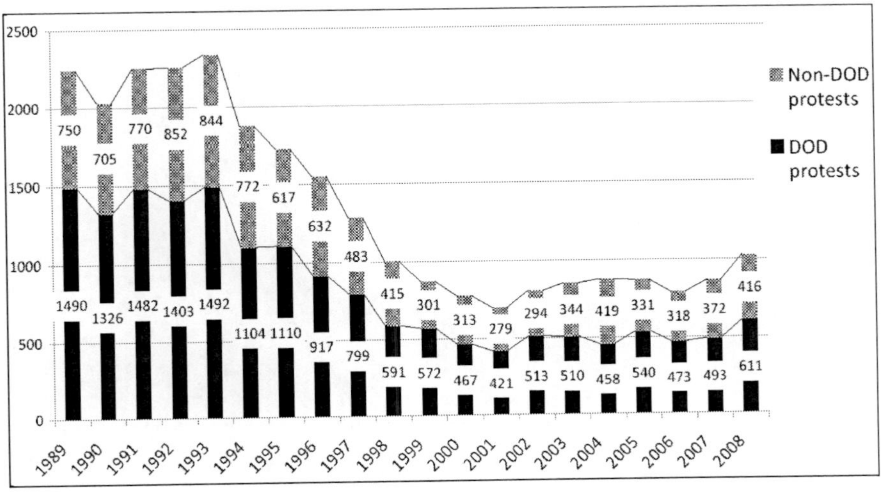

Figure 1. Number of Protest Filed 1989- FY 2008

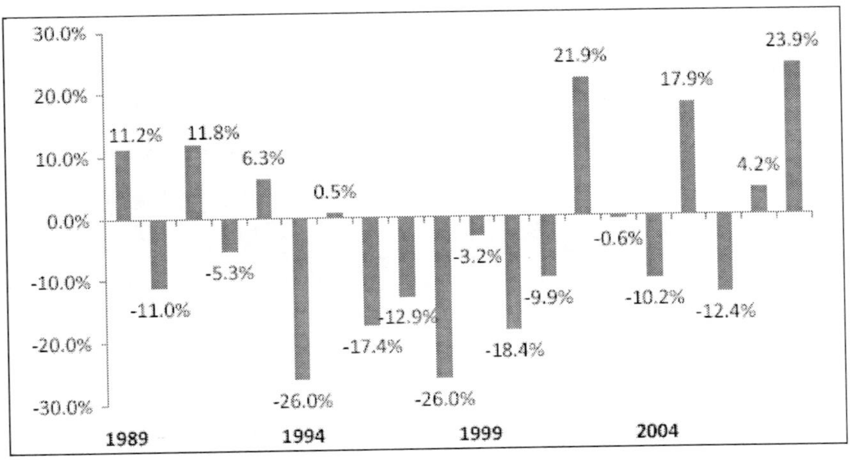

Figure 2. Percent Change in Number of DOD Protests Filed Year to Year FY 1989 – FY 2008

Examining only the past 5 years (Figures 3 and 4), the variability in DOD protest filings, on a year-to-year basis, has swung up and down--just as the totals of such filings have varied over the past 20 years.

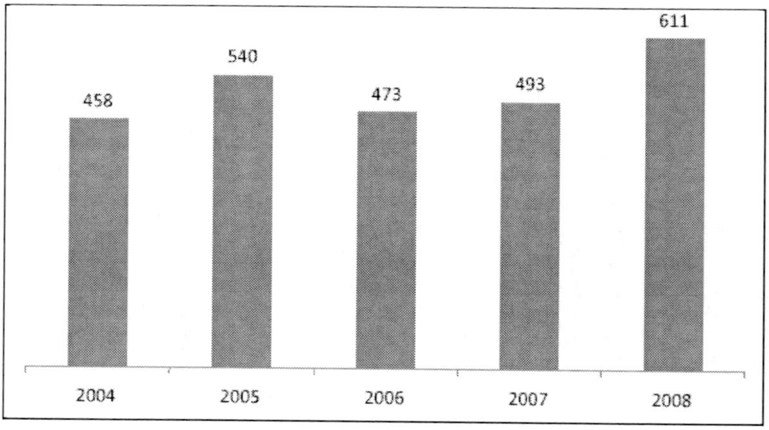

Figure 3. Number of DOD Protests Filed FY 2004 – FY 2008

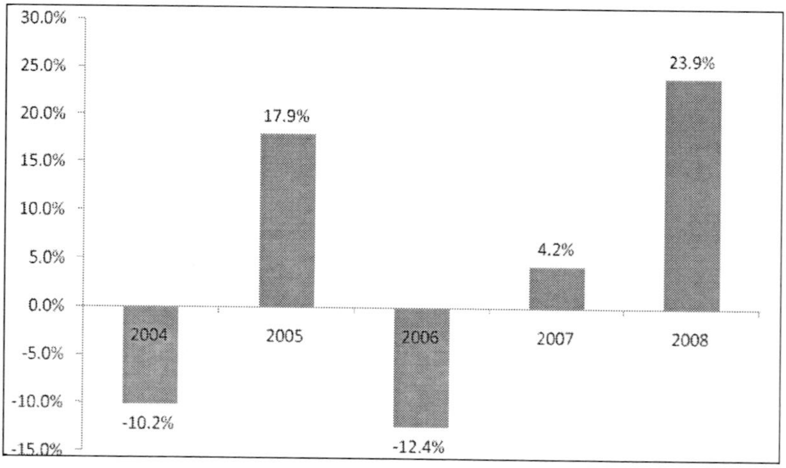

Figure 4. Precent change in DOD Protests FY 2004 – FY 2008

The number of filings in the 4-year period from FY 2004 to FY 2007 ranged between 458-540 per year, with an average of 491 protests filed. In FY 2008 there was a significant increase in the number of DOD protests filed. Specifically, FY 2008 brought an increase of 118 DOD protests over the previous year, to 611 (a 23.9 percent increase). A portion of this increase (30 protests, or about 25 percent of the increase in filings) was tied to recent statutory expansions of GAO's bid protest jurisdiction. As a result of the statutory changes, GAO now considers protests concerning task and delivery orders issued after May 27, 2008, provided they are valued at more than $10 million.[9] In addition, section 326 of the NDAA increased the scope of GAO's bid protest review with respect to public-private competitions conducted pursuant to OMB Circular No. A-76.[10] After removing the portion of the increase related to statutory changes in jurisdiction, FY 2008 saw an increase of 88 DOD protests, to 581 (an increase of 17.8 percent over FY 2007).

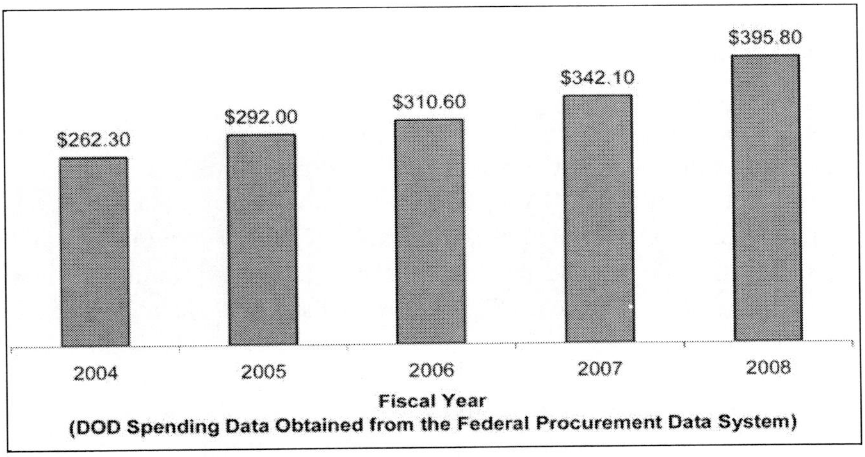

Figure 5. DOD Procurement Spending (in billions) Adjusted for Inflation

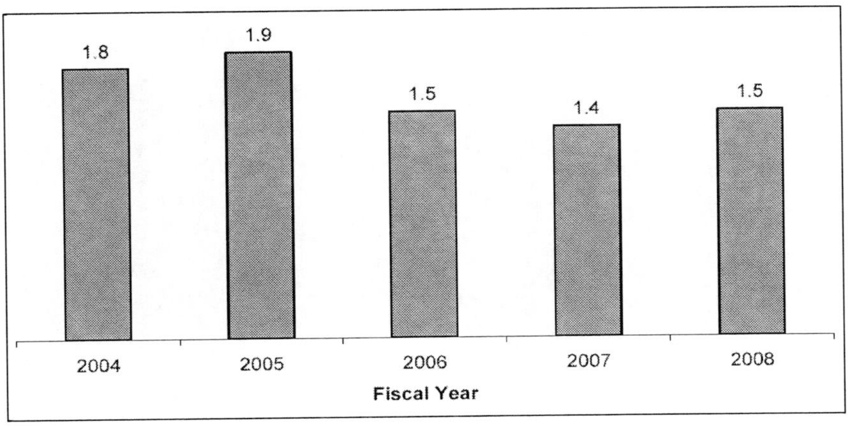

Figure 6. Number of DOD Protests Filed per Billion DOD Procurement Dollars Spent

The somewhat higher number of DOD procurements protested to GAO (up 17.8 percent in FY 2008 after removing protests resulting from statutory changes) needs to be put in the context of the increase in DOD procurement spending over the past few years. From FY 2007 to FY 2008 alone, DOD procurement spending increased 15.7 percent (Figure 5). These similar rates of increase may suggest that the increase in protests was due in part to DOD's increase in procurement spending. *See GAO Bid Protests: Trends, Analysis, and Options for Congress*, Congressional Research Service, Feb. 11, 2009, at 7 (suggesting that "the recent rise in protests is primarily a result of increased government contracting activity").

The amount of DOD procurement spending over the past several years also can be correlated to the number of GAO protests of DOD procurements during those years. The result can be shown as a ratio of protests to procurement dollars. In Figure 6, we show that there have been between 1.4 and 1.9 protests filed at GAO for every billion dollars spent by DOD. Importantly, as shown in Figure 6, the number of GAO protests per billion dollars of DOD procurement spending reflects a slight downward trend during this period. In fact the recent CRS review of the GAO bid protest process shows that the number of GAO protests filed between FY 2001 and FY 2008, relative to federal procurement spending, reflects a downward trend in the number of protests filed. *See GAO Bid Protests: Trends, Analysis, and Options for Congress,* Congressional Research Service, Feb. 11, 2009, at 6-7.

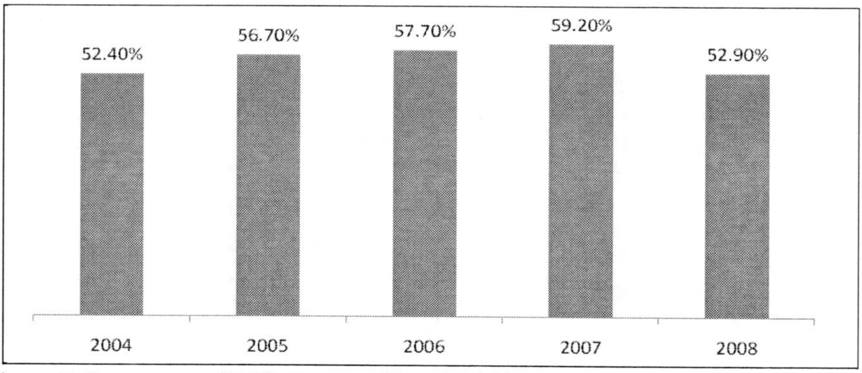

Figure 7. Percentage of DOD Protests Closed Within 30 Days

Despite the variability in protest filings from one year to the next, our Office minimizes the delay and disruption associated with protest filings by resolving protests as expeditiously as practicable. In fact, during the last 5 years, we have consistently closed more than half of all DOD protests within 30 days of when they were filed (Figure 7).

The vast majority of cases closed within the first 30 days are dismissed because the protest fails to meet one of the threshold tests (such as timeliness) explained above. Another typical basis for dismissal is where the protester withdraws its complaint, often after the agency takes corrective action to remedy the problem protested. In addition, many of our dismissals occur after an agency elects to take corrective action rather than defend its procurement--and where we agree that the corrective action renders the pending protest moot. By resolving more than half of all DOD protests within the first 30 days, our Office helps minimize the delay and disruption that protests can cause to DOD procurements.

"Frivolous and Improper" Protests

In its report, the committee directed GAO to assess the extent to which "frivolous and improper" bid protests may be increasing. Because the report does not specify what is meant by frivolous and improper protests, we have looked to the federal courts for their definition of frivolous legal actions.[11]

The courts have identified two ways in which legal actions may be deemed frivolous. First, a legal action is considered "frivolous as filed" when a plaintiff or appellant grounds its case on arguments or issues "that are beyond the reasonable contemplation of fair-minded people, and no basis for [the party's position] in law or fact can be or is even arguably shown." *Abbs v. Principi,* 237 F.3d 1342, 1345 (Fed. Cir. 2001), *citing State Indus., Inc. v. Mor-Flo Indus., Inc.*, 948 F.2d 1573, 1578 (Fed. Cir. 1991); *see also International Union of Bricklayers Etc. v. Martin Jaska, Inc.*, 752 F.2d 1401, 1406 (9th Cir. 1985) ("frivolous appeal is defined as one in which the result is obvious, or where the appellants' claims are utterly meritless"). Second, a legal action is considered "frivolous as argued" when a plaintiff or appellant has not dealt fairly with the court, has significantly misrepresented the law or facts, or has abused the judicial process by repeatedly litigating the same issue in the same court. *Abbs v. Principi*, 237 F.3d at 1345; *Lawrence N. Sparks v. Eastman-Kodak Co.*, 230 F.3d 1344, 1345 (Fed. Cir. 2000); *see also Finch v. Hughes Aircraft Co.*, 926 F.2d 1574, 1582 (Fed. Cir. 1991).

The courts have repeatedly recognized, however, that a legal action found to be without merit is not necessarily frivolous. *See Abbs v. Principi*, 237 F.3d at 1345. A legal complaint that is poorly drafted, or based on weak facts, is not necessarily frivolous. *Ravens Group, Inc. v. United States,* 79 Fed. Cl. 100, 113 (2007). Likewise, a legal argument that is ultimately incorrect is not necessarily frivolous. *Ravens Group, Inc. v. United States,* 79 Fed. Cl. at 114;

Saladino v. United States, 63 Fed. Cl. 754, 757 (2005); *see also Fed. R. Civ. P. 11* (Advisory Committee Notes on 1993 Amendments).

These judicial decisions show that a frivolous legal action must be more than simply one without merit. Rather, the court cases make it clear that the pursuing party knew, or should have known--either at the time of filing or subsequently--that the legal action was so utterly without merit that it was essentially pursued in bad faith. We think this definition is appropriate for our protest forum as well.

Applying the standards articulated by the courts, the fact that a protest is denied for lack of merit does not necessarily mean that it was frivolous. Likewise, the fact that a protest is dismissed because of a procedural deficiency does not necessarily mean that the protest was frivolous. In our view, even when a protest is dismissed for lack of a valid legal basis, it should not necessarily be considered frivolous; rather, the key question is whether the protest was filed in bad faith.[12] A determination by GAO that a protest is frivolous would require determining not only that the protest is without merit or procedurally defective, but also that the protest is so utterly without merit as to have been filed in bad faith.

GAO does not categorize protests as frivolous, and thus, has not identified as frivolous any protests during the last 5 years involving contract awards made by DOD.[13] That does not mean, however, that meritless protests, or those that a reasonable third party might label frivolous, remain open at GAO, thus delaying DOD procurements. As discussed above, GAO promptly dismisses protests that do not state a valid legal basis or are otherwise procedurally defective, consistent with our broad statutory authority. Thus, GAO dismisses protests, where appropriate, without the need to resolve whether the protest was frivolous.

Concerns with Measures to Disincentivize Protests

The committee directed GAO to address whether the filing of frivolous and improper protests might be disincentivized. We have two interrelated observations in this regard. First, our current procedures permit us to dismiss early in the process a significant number of protests that, for instance, are untimely, fail for lack of standing, or fail to assert a valid legal basis for protest. Our current process, we believe, permits us to identify and dismiss protests that would arguably fall under the rubric "frivolous as filed." Similarly, protests that would arguably fall under the "frivolous as argued" rubric, even were they not dismissed early in the process, would be identified later in the process and dismissed or denied as appropriate at that point. Accordingly, given our current broad authority to expeditiously dispose of a protest that does not merit further consideration and development, we do not believe that GAO requires any additional authority to dismiss protests, nor are we seeking such authority. Our second observation is that attempts to disincentivize protests that in some sense might be considered frivolous may have, on balance, the unintended consequence of harming the federal procurement system by discouraging participation in federal contracting and, in turn, limiting competition.

Imposing penalties for protesting--such as fines, a requirement to reimburse agency litigation costs, or the inclusion of a vendor's protest track record in past performance evaluations--as a means to disincentivize frivolous protests could have serious negative consequences for contractors (particularly small businesses), our Office, and the procurement process. Importantly, any system that imposes penalties on contractors for filing frivolous protests would require adequate due process protections to avoid punishing a company for filing a good-faith but unmeritorious protest.[14]

As a general matter, a determination that a protest is frivolous would require an additional inquiry beyond our current practice of determining whether a protest meets the threshold requirements for filing a protest, and then determining the merits of that protest. Specifically, finding that a protest is frivolous would require a determination that the protest was brought in bad faith--an assessment of the subjective intent of the protester. Such a fact-specific inquiry could require substantial litigation, such as declarations, affidavits, or live testimony, to assess whether the protester possessed the intent required for our Office to conclude that its protest was filed in bad faith.

In our experience, there are many instances in which protesters may file a protest in good faith that is nonetheless based on either a misunderstanding of the facts or misapprehension of the law. This may occur more commonly with small business protesters or protesters not represented by counsel.[15] We think that a careful examination of a protester's subjective intent to distinguish between good faith and bad faith arguments would require a significant diversion of our Office's limited resources--resources currently used to resolve protests as expeditiously as possible.

In addition to the resource implications for our Office, a system of penalties for frivolous protests could impose substantial costs on contractors and agencies. An inquiry into the subjective intent of a protester would require the protester to mount a potentially costly defense in order to avoid either a financial penalty, or the potentially more damaging sanction of a negative past performance rating in future competitions. The required defense could, again, potentially place a disproportionately high burden on small businesses.

Attempts to disincentivize protests ignore several valuable benefits of the current protest process. First, protesters act as "private attorneys general" who use the protest process to identify and pursue complaints concerning the procurement system, with a resultant benefit to the public.[16] In addition, protests provide a form of indirect congressional oversight of the procurement process. *Ameron, Inc. v. U.S. Army Corps of Engineers*, 809 F.2d 979, 984 (3d Cir. 1987) ("the bid protest resolution process created by CICA is also intended to inform Congress of the operation of existing procurement laws, and to use the pressure of publicity to enforce compliance with those laws … [by enabling] disappointed bidders to compel the executive to explain some of its procurement decisions to the Comptroller General").

In our view, potential penalties--along with the additional litigation necessary to establish the *sine qua non* for the imposition of penalties, namely, bad faith--risk discouraging good-faith protests. In addition, protests bring an important element of transparency and accountability into the federal procurement system that otherwise might be unavailable. Protests also provide guidance to agencies in the form of publicly-available decisions interpreting procurement laws and regulations.

Finally, the imposition of penalties on protesters could result in a chilling effect on the participation of contractors in both the protest process and federal procurement as a whole. As the conference report accompanying CICA stated, the availability of a strong bid protest mechanism promotes competition in the procurement system by providing contractors a measure of confidence that concerns regarding potentially unfair treatment may be addressed in a neutral forum.[17] Contractors, particularly small businesses, could conclude that the risk of being penalized for a good-faith protest--or the potential that they may have to litigate whether their protest was frivolous--outweighs the potential benefit in filing the protest. Contractors might also perceive the inclusion of penalties in GAO's statutory mandate as an indication that protests have become disfavored as a matter of policy. To the extent contractors believe that it is less likely that their legitimate concerns will be addressed, the result could be an increased distrust of the U.S. procurement system and reduced participation in the system--especially by small businesses. Either of these outcomes could reduce competition and impair the government's ability to obtain the best value in procuring goods and services.

Conclusion

GAO's existing bid protest process provides a balanced approach to adjudicate and resolve challenges brought by protesters to federal government procurements. Our existing regulations and procedures permit us to promptly close protests that do not merit further development. We do not believe that GAO requires additional authority to dismiss protests, and we are not seeking such further authority. In fact, attempts to disincentivize frivolous protests could introduce significant unintended consequences into the current system, by adding substantial costs and discouraging good-faith protests. As Congress has recognized, a robust bid protest process brings an important element of transparency and accountability into the federal procurement system and ultimately promotes competition by ensuring that concerns about unfair treatment will be addressed in a neutral forum. As our extensive track record shows, GAO currently has, and effectively uses, the tools necessary to continue our key role in the bid protest process, with due consideration of both agencies' needs to proceed with their procurements and the need to provide an avenue of meaningful relief to protesters.

We hope you find this information useful. Should you have any questions, please contact Michael R. Golden, Managing Associate General Counsel, at 202-512-8233.

Sincerely yours,

Gary L. Kepplinger
General Counsel

End Notes

[1] H.R. Rep. No. 98-1157, at 23 (1984).

[2] *Id.* at 24.

[3] *Amdahl Corp.; ViON Corp.*, B-212018, B-212018.2, July 1, 1983, 83-2 CPD ¶ 51.

[4] *Amdahl Corp.; ViON Corp.--Recon.*, B-212018.3, B-212018.4, Dec. 19, 1983, 83-2 CPD ¶ 703.

[5] *Competition in Contracting Act of 1984: Hearing on H.R. 5184 Before the House Committee on Government Operations*, 98th Congress. 59-60 (1984) (statement of A.G.W. Biddle, President, Computer and Communications Industry Association).

[6] Because GAO is not a court, it cannot (unlike the Court of Federal Claims) direct executive-branch agencies to take corrective action. Instead, GAO makes recommendations. Except in rare instances, these recommendations are routinely followed. *See* GAO Annual Reports to Congress on Bid Protests for Fiscal Years 1986-2008. (The annual reports for FY 1995-2008 are available on GAO's website, *www.gao.gov*.)

[7] Because we were asked about protests of DOD procurements, this chapter generally refers only to DOD procurements. In many cases, the analysis and our conclusions would be the same for civilian agency procurements. In any event, no inference should be drawn that protest processes or trends would be different for civilian agency procurements.

[8] CICA requires GAO to report to Congress each year on the number of protests filed. GAO's long-standing approach to this requirement has been to report the docket numbers ("B" numbers, such as B-123456) assigned by our Office, not the number of procurements challenged. Thus, where a protester files a supplemental protest or multiple parties protest the same procurement action, multiple iterations of the same "B" number are assigned (e.g., B-123456.2, B-123456.3). These docket numbers accurately reflect GAO's protest filings, but they overstate the number of procurements challenged. In contrast, in recent testimony by the Secretary of Defense, DOD characterized the effect of the protest process in terms of the number of procurement actions challenged. For purposes of this chapter, we are adopting DOD's recent approach. Thus, for purposes of counting the number of protests filed, we eliminated from our count multiple iterations of the same "B" number. As a consequence, the number of protests in this chapter reflects the number of procurements challenged in a given fiscal year.

[9] In this regard, section 843 of the National Defense Authorization Act for Fiscal Year 2008 (NDAA), Pub. L. No. 110-181, 122 Stat. 3 (2008), amended 10 U.S.C. § 2304c and 41 U.S.C. § 253j to authorize GAO to hear protests of the award or proposed award of certain task and delivery orders under indefinite-delivery/indefinite-quantity contracts.

[10] NDAA, Pub. L. No. 110-181, § 326, 122 Stat. 3 (2008), amending 31 U.S.C. § 3551.

[11] For purposes of this chapter, we regard the terms "frivolous" and "improper" as, in essence, interchangeable.

[12] We think there is no dispute that a protest should not be viewed as frivolous where the protest is sustained, or where the agency takes corrective action rather than defend the procurement.

[13] Similarly, contracting agencies themselves rarely describe protests as frivolous. For example, the last reported GAO decision in which a contracting agency (the Air Force) characterized a protest as frivolous occurred in 1996. *See Bionetics Corp.--Costs,* B-270323.3, Aug. 16, 1996, 96-2 CPD ¶ 70. Undercutting the agency's position in that case is the fact that, after the agency initially asked GAO to dismiss as "frivolous" the protester's assertion that the agency had improperly deviated from the evaluation scheme set forth in the solicitation, the agency subsequently decided to take corrective action after acknowledging that its evaluation scheme was, in fact, flawed.

[14] *E.g., Old Dominion Dairy Products, Inc. v. Secretary of Defense*, 631 F.2d 953 (D.C. Cir. 1980).

[15] In keeping with CICA's mandate to provide "for the inexpensive and expeditious resolution of protests," 31 U.S.C. § 3554(a)(1), our regulations do not require protesters to be represented by counsel, and a significant percentage of protesters appear *pro se*.

[16] *See Scanwell Lab., Inc. v. Shaffer*, 424 F.2d 859, 864 (D.C. Cir. 1970) ("Instead of designating the Attorney General, or some other public officer, to bring such proceedings, Congress can constitutionally enact a statute conferring on any nonofficial person, or on a designated group of non-official persons, authority to bring a suit to prevent action by an officer in violation of his statutory powers; for then, in like manner, there is an actual controversy, and there is nothing constitutionally prohibiting Congress from empowering any person, official or not, to institute a proceeding involving such a controversy, even if the sole purpose is to vindicate the public interest. Such persons, so authorized, are, so to speak, private Attorney Generals."); *Department of the Navy--Modification of Remedy*, B-284080.3, May 24, 2000, 2000 CPD ¶ 99 ("In our view, [the] protest served precisely the purpose anticipated by CICA [by] highlight[ing] a failure by GSA to properly maintain the FSS program . . . [W]e think CICA clearly anticipates that the government should reimburse DRS for acting as a private attorney general in shining the light of publicity here."); *E&R, Inc.--Claim for Costs,* B-255868, B-255868.2, May 30, 1996, 96-1 CPD ¶ 264 ("In essence,

entitlement to bid protest costs relieves a protester of the financial demands of acting as a private attorney general where it brings to light an agency's failure to conduct a procurement in accordance with law and regulation.").

[17] H.R. Conf. Rep. No. 98-861, at 1435 (1984), *reprinted in* 1984 U.S.S.C.C.A.N., at 2123.

In: Government Awards and Objections: Bid... ISBN: 978-1-61728-680-3
Editor: Matthew A. Sauter

Chapter 5

GAO: GOVERNMENT ACCOUNTABILITY OFFICE AND GENERAL ACCOUNTING OFFICE*

Frederick M. Kaiser

SUMMARY

On July 7, 2004, an old congressional support agency was given a new name, while keeping the same initials (GAO): at that time, the General Accounting Office, established in 1921, was re-designated the Government Accountability Office (P.L. 108-271). The renaming, which came at the request of its head, the Comptroller General (CG) of the United States, was designed to reflect the agency's evolution and additional duties since its creation more than eight decades before.

The Government Accountability Office is the largest of three agencies that provide staff support, research, review, and analysis for Congress. GAO operates under the control and direction of the Comptroller General, who is appointed by the President, with the advice and consent of the Senate, for a 15-year nonrenewable term. A unique arrangement begins the process with a

---

* This is an edited, reformatted and augmented version of a CRS Report for Congress publication dated September 2008.

special bicameral commission of legislators from both parties making recommendations to the President. The CG post is currently vacant, with the resignation of David Walker on March 12, 2008.

GAO was established in 1921 as an independent auditor of government agencies and activities by the Budget and Accounting Act. The office was intended to be "independent of the executive departments," the entities it would audit and review. Sometimes called "Congress's watchdog" and its "investigative arm," GAO now provides a variety of services to Congress that extend beyond its original functions and duties, including oversight, investigation, review, and evaluation of executive programs, operations, and activities. Several proposals in the 110th Congress are seen as augmenting GAO's capabilities. These include clarifying its audit authority over the Intelligence Community (H.R. 978 and S. 82) and enhancing its powers to gain access to executive documents (H.R. 6388). In a separate matter, personnel flexibilities powers granted to the Comptroller General in 2004 have generated some controversy in Congress and among GAO employees. As an outgrowth of this and other considerations, GAO staff have set up a new bargaining unit, the first union in the office's history. Legislation has also been proposed that would, among other things, amend GAO's basic authority over personnel and pay matters for employees, provide pay adjustments and reimbursements for certain employees who had not received pay increases in 2006 and 2007, and establish an office of inspector general (H.R. 5683, which has passed the House and Senate and been sent to the President).

Throughout much of its history, the office has experienced growth in its powers, duties, and resources. In the mid-1990s, however, it was the subject of congressional hearings, studies, and proposals for change, connected with its mission, roles, and capabilities; these reviews were generated in part by criticisms of its perceived orientation. As a result, GAO's budget and personnel levels were reduced and certain of the "executive powers" of the Comptroller General. In comparison to these earlier budget reductions, however, the office's funding has since risen, from $358 million in FY1998 to $507.2 million in FY2008. Nonetheless, GAO's staff size (at 3,100 in FY2008) has remained lower than in earlier years.

This chapter will be updated as developments dictate.

INTRODUCTION

The Government Accountability Office (GAO) — with more than 3,100 staff positions and an annual budget exceeding $507 million in FY2008 — is the largest of several support agencies that provide research, review, and analysis for Congress; and it is the only one with a nationwide field structure.[1] GAO, which had been titled the General Accounting Office until 2004, operates under the control and direction of the Comptroller General of the United States (CG). The head is appointed by the President — after receiving recommendations from a special bicameral congressional commission — by and with the advice and consent of the Senate, for a 15-year nonrenewable term. The position, which had been vacant for two years, was filled in late 1998, when David M. Walker was sworn in and became only the seventh Comptroller General in GAO's history, which began more than eight decades ago. The post is now vacant with Mr. Walker's resignation on March 12, 2008.[2]

GAO was established as an independent auditor of government agencies and activities by the Budget and Accounting Act of 1921 (42 Stat. 23). That enactment also created the Bureau of the Budget, the forerunner to the Office of Management and Budget, and established presidential authority over the budget formulation process. The basic authority for the office and its head is codified at 31 U.S.C. 701 et seq. and 3511 et seq. Numerous other statutory provisions affect the powers and duties of both GAO and the CG.

The office was designed to be "independent of the executive departments," which were placed under its audit and review powers (31 U.S.C. 702(a)). Sometimes characterized as "Congress's watchdog" and the "investigative arm of Congress," the GAO provides a variety of services to Congress, largely connected to the oversight, investigation, and evaluation of executive operations, activities, and programs.

The evolution of the office's authority, functions, and mandates over time, along with new pay and personnel powers for the Comptroller General, prompted him to request a change in its name: from the General Accounting Office to the Government Accountability Office (P.L. 108-271). GAO's current activities and services include:[3]

- auditing and evaluating federal programs and operations;
- conducting special investigations (through a small office) of alleged violations of federal criminal law, particularly conflict of interest or procurement and contract fraud;

- providing various legal services to Congress, including advice on legal issues involving government programs and activities;
- resolving bid protests that challenge government contract awards;
- prescribing accounting principles and standards for the executive branch, advising federal agencies on fiscal and other policies and procedures, and setting standards for auditing government programs;
- assisting the professional audit/evaluation community in improving and keeping abreast of ongoing developments in such matters as audit methodology and approaches; and
- detailing GAO staff to work directly for congressional committees (in these temporary transfers, the assigned staffs represent the committees and not GAO itself).[4]

Since 1994, GAO has been the subject of congressional hearings, studies, and proposals for change connected with its mission, roles, capabilities, and personnel system. After a lengthy period of growth — in its powers, duties, and resources —the office experienced reductions in these areas in the mid-1990s. In 1996, for instance, certain of the "executive powers" of the Comptroller General were abolished or transferred to executive branch agencies. In addition, GAO's budget was cut by 25% over a two-year period (FY1996 and FY1997), representing the largest reduction in a seven-year downsizing (1992-1999). Since then, however, its budget authority has increased, from a low of $358 million in FY1998 to a high of $507.2 million for FY2008. Since 1995, however, full-time-equivalent employees are fewer than in each previous year, with 3,100 currently compared to 4,324 in FY1995. In fact, in the midst of the cutbacks during the 1990s, GAO experienced an overall staff reduction of 39% from FY1992 to FY1998.

Establishment and Evolution of GAO

1921 Establishment

The Budget and Accounting Act of 1921, which created the General Accounting Office, built upon efforts over a considerable period of time to develop a new budget process and involved trade-offs between the legislature and executive.[5] The legislation gave the President substantial responsibilities and authority over the federal budget formulation process. To assist in this endeavor, the statute also created the Bureau of the Budget in the Treasury Department. (The bureau was later moved to the Executive Office of the President and is now known as the Office of Management and Budget.) As a counterweight to these enhancements of executive power in the budget process, Congress established the General Accounting Office in the legislative branch, in large part through the transfer of comptroller and auditor duties from the Treasury Department.

Congressional work on what was to become the 1921 act began two years earlier with legislative proposals to transfer the duties and responsibilities of the comptrollers and auditors from the Treasury Department to an entity independent of the executive departments and, indeed, located in the legislative branch. This initial legislation was vetoed by President Woodrow Wilson, who objected to a section allowing for the removal of the new Comptroller General by Congress alone, through a concurrent resolution.[6] This provision was later changed to allow for the removal of the Comptroller General by adoption of a joint resolution. The joint resolution, which must be signed by the President, is subject to presidential veto and the possibility of a veto override.

The 1921 act abolished the post of Comptroller and Assistant Comptroller of the Treasury, along with the six auditors in the department. Their personnel, records, and resources were transferred to the new General Accounting Office. The establishing authority also vested GAO with the powers and responsibilities of the auditors and Comptroller of the Treasury, some of which dated to the Treasury Act of 1789.

Along with this, the originating legislation gave the Comptroller General broad authority to "investigate, at the seat of government or elsewhere, all matters relating to the receipt, disbursement, and application of public funds" (42 Stat. 25). To augment this, the Comptroller General was given extensive access to information in "all departments and establishments ... regarding the powers, duties, activities, organization, financial transactions, and methods of business of their respective office as he may from time to time require" (42 Stat. 26).

Adding to the new position, the law authorized the Comptroller General to recommend legislation "to facilitate the prompt and accurate rendition and settlement of accounts and concerning such other matters relating to the receipt, disbursement, and application of public funds as he may think advisable" (42 Stat. 25-26). The initial authority, moreover, established new requirements for reporting to Congress and directed the Comptroller General to make special investigations and reports when ordered by either House of

Congress or by any committee with jurisdiction over revenue, appropriations, and expenditures.

Expansion and Extension of Authority and Jurisdiction

Since 1921, the scope of GAO's powers, mandates, and jurisdiction has been expanded by public laws. Its current functions, duties, and extensive jurisdiction (with a few notable exceptions[7]) have grown out of its powers over finances and expenditures of the federal government, the two major legislative branch reorganizations (in 1946 and 1970), and specific additions to the Comptroller General's responsibilities and authority.

Additional Responsibilities

Additional responsibilities and authority have accrued over time.

Audit and Accounting Authority

The Government Corporation Control Act of 1945, for instance, granted GAO audit authority over mixed-ownership government corporations (59 Stat. 600-601). And the Budget and Accounting Procedures Act of 1950 directed the Comptroller General to prescribe principles and standards for accounting in executive agencies (64 Stat. 835). Building on this, the Federal Manager's Financial Integrity Act of 1982 required each agency to establish internal accounting and administrative controls in accordance with standards prescribed by the Comptroller General (96 Stat. 814). In addition, the Chief Financial Officers Act of 1990 gave the Comptroller General enhanced audit authority and the power to review financial audits conducted by an inspector general or an external auditor (104 Stat. 2852-2854).

GPRA

Along these same lines, GAO has a prominent role in monitoring and reviewing the development and implementation of the Government Performance and Results Act of 1993 (GPRA) (107 Stat. 285).[8] GAO has been involved not only in the training of executive personnel and congressional staff who are to implement and oversee GPRA, but also in the evaluation of pilot programs, strategic plans, annual performance plans and goals, and followup reports from the agencies.

Reviewing Regulations

In the 106th Congress, GAO was authorized to review federal agency rules and regulations, under the Truth in Regulating Act of 2000. But the program was not implemented because of a lack of funding.[9]

Access to Government Documents and Information

In order to fulfill its mission, the Government Accountability Office has been given broad powers to gain access to information and materials of government entities, based on its original authority as well as later supplements (31 U.S.C. 712 and 716), with several exceptions. These powers are designed to provide access — fully and directly in most cases — or, barring that, provide an auxiliary means to compel recalcitrant offices to release information. To enforce this, the Comptroller General has power, rarely used, to sue a noncomplying agency for the production of requested records (31 U.S.C. 716). Under this authority, the CG makes a written request to the agency head, who has 20 days to explain why the records are not being made available. At that time, the Comptroller General may file a report with the President, the Director of the Office of Management and Budget, the head of the relevant agency, and Congress. Twenty days after this action, the CG may file suit in the district court for the District of Columbia to require the agency head to produce the requested records.

An attempt to use this authority in 2001 resulted in a conflict with the executive. In this case, the Comptroller General was denied access to records of an executive commission — the National Energy Policy Development Group (NEPDG), established by a presidential memorandum and headed by the Vice President.[10] Still denied access after issuing a demand letter, the Comptroller General sued. In 2002, however, the District Court for the District of Columbia held in *Walker v. Cheney* that GAO lacked standing to sue the Vice President to compel the release of information pertaining to NEPDG. The decision has not been appealed. Legislation (H.R. 6388) has been introduced in the 110th Congress — by Representative Henry Waxman, chairman of the House Committee on Oversight and Government Reform, for himself and 18 other House chairs — that would, in effect, override *Walker v. Cheney*, by augmenting the CG's authority to gain access to such records.[11] The bill would also affirm GAO's right to obtain records from three specified agencies (i.e., Centers for Medicare and Medicaid Services, Federal Trade Commission, and Food and Drug Administration). Furthermore, H.R. 6388 would expand GAO's authority to administer oaths and give it express powers to interview federal employees when conducting evaluations and investigations.

Legislative Reorganization Act Changes

Major legislative reorganization efforts have also augmented GAO's powers and independence. The Legislative Reorganization Act (LRA) of 1946 specifically directed the Comptroller General "to make an expenditure analysis of each agency in the executive branch of Government (including Government corporations), which, in the opinion of the Comptroller General, will enable Congress to determine whether public funds have been economically and efficiently administered and expended" (60 Stat. 837). In the 1970 LRA, Congress significantly expanded GAO's assistance to congressional committees and strengthened its program evaluation responsibilities (84 Stat. 1167-1171).

Other Duties Assigned to the Comptroller General

In addition to the office's assignments and powers, the Comptroller General himself has been given a variety of specific responsibilities in public law, some of which are temporary while others are permanent. Over the years, these have included the power to bring suit to require the release of impounded funds (2 U.S.C. 687); a duty to impose civil penalties under the Energy Policy and Conservation Act of 1975 (42 U.S.C. 6385(a)); the assignments to serve as a member of the Chrysler Corporation Loan Guarantee Board (15 U.S.C. 1862) and of the Board of Directors of the United States Railway Association (45 U.S.C. 711(d)); and the authority to consider bid protests under the Competition in Contracting Act of 1984 (31 U.S.C. 3551-3556).

The Comptroller General, along with the Secretary of the Treasury and Director of OMB, serves as a principal on the Federal Accounting Standards Advisory Board. It considers and recommends issuance of accounting standards and principles and provides interpretations of existing ones. Previously, the CG had co-chaired the Cost Accounting Standards Review Panel, consisting of public officials and defense industry representatives. It had examined operations and activities of the Cost Accounting Standards Board (CASB), an executive agency in OMB (41 U.S.C. 422).

In the aftermath of the devastating Gulf Coast hurricanes of 2005, the Comptroller General joined inspectors general from appropriate agencies in a new Hurricane Katrina Contract Audit Task Force. It serves as a means of coordinating the efforts of federal organizations auditing the Gulf Coast Recovery Program. Besides GAO, these include offices of inspector general in the Departments of Defense, Homeland Security, Housing and Urban Development, Health and Human Services, and Transportation, as well as the Environmental Protection Agency and General Services Administration.

The Comptroller General also chaired the Commercial Activities Panel (CAP), a now-defunct interagency group consisting of representatives from executive departments (i.e., the Office of Personnel Management and Department of Defense), as well as from private organizations and public sector unions. The congressionally mandated panel, which completed its mission in 2002, studied and made recommendations for improving the policies and procedures governing the transfer of commercial activities from the government to contractor personnel.[12]

Changes in Authority

Several different types of changes in the authority of GAO and the CG have occurred since the mid-1980s.

In 1985, a constitutional conflict arose over powers delegated to the Comptroller General, when Congress gave him specific budget-reduction authority under the Balanced Budget and Deficit Control Act.[13] The CG was to review recommendations about such reductions and report his findings to the President, who, in turn, was to issue a sequestration order mandating spending reductions specified by the CG. Additional legislative mechanisms (or "fallback" provisions) to cut spending were also included in the statute. The Supreme Court held, however, that the delegation of authority to the CG was unconstitutional, concluding that "the powers vested in the Comptroller General under section 251 violate the command of the Constitution that the Congress play no direct role in the execution of the laws."[14]

In contrast to GAO's long-term expansion over decades, the mid-1990s witnessed a cutback in its authority and, perhaps more importantly, its resources (discussed below). The 1996 General Accounting Office Act abolished or transferred — to the Director of the Office of Management and Budget or the head of an executive department or agency — certain specific "executive" powers of the Comptroller General (110 Stat. 3826 and 3838-3840). These related to his authority to make certain determinations about executive assistance and services, resolve disputes over certain purchases made by executive agencies, conduct identified audits of executive accounts, or prescribe regulations for specified executive operations.

Proposed Changes for GAO in the 110th Congress

A number of proposals in the 110th Congress would affect GAO's organization, structure, and authority.

Structure and Organization

In July 2007, the Comptroller General called for changes in a number of areas, changes that have been included, as requested or modified, in legislative proposals in the 110th Congress. The initial version of the Government Accountability Office Act, H.R. 3268, was introduced at the request of the CG; and an amended version, H.R. 5683, has passed the House and Senate and has been sent to the White House.[15] The various transformations would affect GAO's pay and personnel system, retirement pay, voluntary separation incentive payments, the CG's annuity level, reimbursement of audit costs, administering oaths, appointment of the deputy, and the office of inspector general.

Pay and Benefits

If signed into law, H.R. 5683 would modify the CG's authority over pay rates for GAO officers and employees. One provision, for instance, would allow them to rise to level III of the Executive Schedule (EX), instead of the current GS-15 ceiling, while another would grant more discretion to the Comptroller General in determining pay for several high-ranking positions now paid by reference to the EX Schedule; these posts are the Comptroller General, deputy, general counsel, and up to 20 experts and consultants. The legislation would also set new requirements for future annual pay adjustments and respond to past pay discrepancies. With regard to the latter, a proposal would grant pay adjustments for certain employees and officers, including a lump-sum payment for officers and employees who failed to receive certain pay increases in 2006 and 2007. Another modification, in H.R. 3268 but not H.R. 5638, would set the Comptroller General's annuity at EX level II. (Discussed further below.)

Deputy Comptroller General's Appointment

The appointment process for the Deputy Comptroller General would be transformed — under H.R. 3268 but not H.R. 5683 — allowing the

Comptroller General to appoint the deputy, after consultation with a special congressional commission. The new process would end the current arrangement in which the deputy, whose post has been vacant for nearly 30 years, is a presidential nominee subject to Senate confirmation.

Inspector General

The establishment of a statutory inspector general (IG), also contained in H.R. 5683, would replace the current administrative construct. The new office would mirror but not duplicate its counterparts in "designated federal entities" — usually the smaller agencies, boards, commissions, foundations, and government corporations, where the IG is appointed by and can be removed by the agency head — now operating under the Inspector General Act of 1978, as amended.[16] The new statutory inspector general at GAO, to be selected without regard to political affiliation, would be appointed by and removable by the Comptroller General, who could not, however, prevent the IG from carrying out his or her duties. The inspector general would be responsible for combating waste, fraud, and abuse in GAO and keeping the Comptroller General and Congress currently and fully informed concerning such matters, by way of semi-annual reports and otherwise. Statutory offices of inspector general, incidently, have previously been established in four other legislative branch entities: the Architect of the Capitol Office, Government Printing Office, Library of Congress, and U.S. Capitol Police, all of which allow for the agency head (or a board) to appoint and remove the inspector general.

Reimbursement of Certain Audit Costs

Another provision in H.R. 5683 calls for the reimbursement of certain audit costs by executive agencies (or components thereof), beginning in FY2009. They would have to reimburse GAO for its costs associated with auditing their annual financial statements or related schedules prepared under 31 U.S.C. 3515 — which covers all accounts and associated activities — under certain conditions. The revenue from the reimbursements would be deposited in a special account in the Treasury, to be made available to GAO as specified in its annual appropriations acts.

Access to Government Records and Information

A conflict with the executive arose in 2001 over GAO's independent access to certain executive branch records, in this case, those of the National Energy Policy Development Group, headed by the Vice President. In 2002, as noted above, a federal district court in *Cheney v. Walker* held that GAO lacked access to the records.[17] In response, Representative Henry Waxman, for himself and 18 other chairs, introduced the Government Accountability Act of 2008 (H.R. 6388) that would augment the CG's power to gain access to such records as well as those from three specified agencies (Centers for Medicare and Medicaid Services, Food and Drug Administration, and Federal Trade Commission).[18] The legislation, which has been approved by the House, would also expand GAO's authority to administer oaths and give it express powers to interview federal employees when conducting evaluations and investigations. Another provision in the bill creates a reporting mechanism, so that Congress would be informed when federal agencies fail to cooperate with the office.

Auditing of the Intelligence Community

As noted above, the Government Accountability Office possess nearly unfettered jurisdiction to audit and investigate the federal government. GAO's access, however, may be precluded in certain situations: by the President, if it involves sensitive or classified records, such as foreign intelligence and counterintelligence activities; in instances where the records are statutorily exempted from disclosure (31 U.S.C. 716(d)); or in cases where an executive agency holds competing powers which prevent GAO access.[19]

The last of these proscriptions has led to conflicts between the Government Accountability Office and the Intelligence Community (IC), particularly the Central Intelligence Agency (CIA).[20] Legislation has been introduced in the 110th Congress to clarify GAO's auditing the IC, with hearings held in 2008.[21]

The CIA views its own statutory authority as keeping it off-limits to independent GAO audits and investigations. Under its interpretation, the CIA has declined to participate in GAO reviews (as well as in some congressional oversight hearings held by panels other than the Select Committees on Intelligence). Other IC components, however, have not asserted the same proscription to GAO audits. In contrast to the CIA's stand, for instance, the Department of Defense has issued the following instructions:

> It is DoD policy that the Department of Defense cooperate fully with the GAO and respond constructively to, and take appropriate corrective action on the basis of, GAO reports .... [But DoD is also to] be alert to identify errors of fact or erroneous interpretation in GAO reports, and to articulate the DoD position in such matters, as appropriate.[22]

GAO has taken exception to the CIA's position, emphasizing that the Office has authority to audit the Agency independently but lacks enforcement power.[23] If enacted, the Intelligence Community Audit Act would change this situation. These and similar proposals, which were first raised in the mid-1970s, are designed to "reaffirm the authority of the Comptroller General to audit and evaluate the programs, activities, and financial transactions of the intelligence community."[24]

GAO Resources

GAO's budget and staffing levels have varied since the mid-1990s, experiencing both downs and ups, with a current leveling off as continuing resolutions have tended to stabilize both figures.

The Government Accountability Office, like the other congressional support agencies, operates under a permanent authorization and an annual appropriation. A proposal in 1994, based on the recommendations of the Joint Committee on the Organization of Congress, would have mandated an eight-year authorization period for all congressional support agencies to replace their permanent authorizations.[25] No action, however, was taken on the recommendation.

Table 1 provides statistics on total new budget authority (gross) and on full-time equivalent employees (FTEs) for GAO from FY1995 through FY2009 (requested).

Table 1. GAO Resources, FY1995-FY2009

Fiscal Year	Total New Budget Authority (gross) (in millions of dollars)	FTEs[c]
2009[a]	545.5	3,251
2008	507.2[b]	3,100[c]
2007	488.6	3,152
2006	488	3,194
2005	475	3,215
2004	468	3,224
2003	458	3,269
2002	436	3,210
2001	405	3,110
2000	380	3,275
1999	368	3,275
1998	358	3,245
1997	359	3,341
1996	379	3,677
1995	448	4,342

a. The FY2009 amounts are GAO's requests in its budget submission to Congress: GAO, *Fiscal Year 2009 Budget Request: U.S. Government Accountability Office*, GAO-08-616T, April 10, 2008, pp. 1 and 5. An earlier request of $549 million was included in the President's budget submission: U.S. Office of Management and Budget (OMB), *Budget of the United States Government for Fiscal Year 2009, Appendix*, (Washington: GPO, 2008), p. 47. For additional information on annual appropriations for GAO and the Legislative Branch, see CRS Report RL34490, *Legislative Branch: FY2009 Appropriations*, by Ida A. Brudnick.

b. P.L. 110-161, Consolidated Appropriations Act for FY2008, Division H, provides $501 million in direct appropriations plus $7.5 million in transfers, for a total of $508.5 million. An across-the-board rescission of 0.25% reduces this amount by $1.27 million, leaving $507.2 million for FY2008. See GAO, *Fiscal Year 2009 Budget Request*, p. 5.

c. Full-time equivalent employees (FTEs) are the maximum number of such positions authorized. The number of actual on-duty employees at any one time may be larger than the FTEs, because of part-time employment of some. Alternatively, the total of on-duty staff may be fewer than the FTEs, because of pre-hiring requirements, retirements, resignations, and/or insufficient funding to reach the authorized level. The FY2008 figure of 3,100 is the number GAO has estimated. OMB, *FY 2009 Budget, Appendix*, p. 47.

Budget Levels

GAO's budget authority and personnel levels have fluctuated since the mid-1990s. At that time, the office experienced a substantial cut in its funding, with a combined 25% reduction in total new budget authority for fiscal years 1996 and 1997, by comparison to its FY1995 total. This continued a downward trend that had begun in FY1992 and ebbed in FY1998. Since then, GAO's budget level has risen each year. And over the past decade, it has increased nearly 30%, from $358 million in FY1998 to $507.2 million in FY2008 and $545.5 million requested for FY2009.

Personnel Levels

In the mid-1990s, GAO also experienced a significant reduction in its personnel levels, as a result of the budget cuts. Because employee compensation constitutes about 80% of GAO's budget, its cost-saving actions resulted in a sizable staff downsizing at the time. According to 1997 testimony by the Acting Comptroller General, the cutbacks "have necessitated a loss of people. Today, as a result of those reductions, GAO staffing is at its lowest level since before World War II."[26]

In 1999, Comptroller General David Walker elaborated on the effects of the seven-year downsizing of GAO (from FY1992 through FY1998). One result was a 39% reduction in its workforce during that span, from 5,325 in FY1992 to 3,245 in FY1998. In 1999 testimony, the CG recounted that the office also

> instituted a reduction-in-force; closed regional offices; imposed a 5-year hiring freeze; eliminated performance rewards; curtailed technology investments; and reduced travel, training, supplies, and other support costs to achieve the overall mandated reduction in spending. GAO is now facing a number of critical human capital, information technology, and work process challenges that it needs to address.[27]

GAO's budget and personnel requests dealt with some of these areas since then. But the office has not seen its staff size exceed the 3,275 FTEs in FY1999 and FY2000; and it witnessed smaller numbers in the two following years (with 3,110 in FY2001 and 3,210 in FY2002). By comparison to these low figures, however, personnel levels rose to 3,269 FTEs in FY2003.

Nonetheless, recent final FTE statistics show a continuing downsizing each year since FY2003 — from 3,269 in that year to 3,100 in FY2008, the lowest total of the past 13 years (see **Table 1**).[28] If approved, the requested number of positions for FY2009 — 3,251 — would reverse this trend.

Personnel System

Legislation enacted in 2004 granted the Comptroller General certain personnel flexibilities over the GAO workforce. This augmented authority from 1980, 1988, and 2000, which provided the basis for the personnel system at GAO.

Antecedent Authority

The General Accounting Office Personnel Act of 1980 was designed to construct an "independent personnel system" (P.L. 96-191, 94 Stat. 27). The new structure replaced GAO's reliance on requirements from several executive branch entities, especially the Office of Personnel Management (OPM) and the Merit System Protection Board. According to the Senate Committee on Governmental Affairs, which reported the proposal favorably, "this independence from regulation by executive branch entities is the principal objective of the legislation."[29] The change, requested by the Comptroller General, was seen as necessary to remove even the appearance of a conflict of interest, as GAO had increased oversight of these agencies and the federal personnel system.[30] This first installment gave the CG authority to "appoint, pay, assign, and direct such personnel as the Comptroller General determines necessary to discharge the duties and functions of the General Accounting Office" (94 Stat. 27). Accompanying this general grant were requirements to meet specified provisions of Title 5 of the *U.S. Code*, which set merit system principles and prohibit certain personnel practices, among other matters (94 Stat. 27).

Amendments to the personnel act were approved in 1988 (P.L. 100-426, 102 Stat. 1598-1602). These revised provisions concerned GAO's personnel appeals board membership and judicial review of its decisions. The amendments also changed the retirement qualifications for the Comptroller General and Deputy, allowing them to remain in office past the otherwise mandatory retirement age of 70; and the statutory changes brought the CG's survivor benefits into conformity with those available to federal judges.

In 2000, the CG's powers over personnel were enhanced through a three-year pilot program allowing for specific personnel flexibilities (P.L. 106-303, 114 Stat. 1063-1070).[31] This legislation gave qualified authority to the Comptroller General to offer certain voluntary separation incentives, along with early retirements, and to implement a reduction in force.

Additional Authority in 2004

The GAO Human Capital Reform Act of 2004 (P.L. 108-271) granted the Comptroller General additional authority over pay and personnel. The enactment allows the Comptroller General to offer early retirement and buy-out incentives; establish an exchange program with the private sector; and make employee relocation benefits more flexible.[32] Another far-reaching provision permits him to set annual pay raises tied more closely with performance appraisal ratings (as opposed to granting automatic yearly increases). In so doing, the CG could also use factors other than the Consumer Price Index, Employment Cost Index, and locality pay surveys to determine the amounts.[33] Other sections, emerging after congressional committee deliberations, are designed to meet several objectives: protect the merit principle of "equal pay for work of equal value," keep the pay rates of employees who have been demoted because of workforce restructuring or job reclassification at their current levels, and set qualifications on exchanges with the private sector.

As described by the Comptroller General, the overall transformation is intended to "further GAO's ability to enhance our performance, assure our accountability, and ensure that we can attract, retain, motivate, and reward a quality and high-performing workforce currently and in future years."[34] Changes in this realm and their source —coming from Congress's largest support agency and its chief examiner of executive personnel systems — attracted widespread attention and considerations of a number of matters connected with it, both favorable and not.

Followup Study and Ongoing Considerations

A followup report —issued in mid-2005 under the auspices of the IBM Center for the Business of Government — provides initial responses to these questions, based on an examination of the changes under GAO's new personnel system.[35]

The report concluded that GAO successfully used human capital management, broadly defined, to drive its organizational transformation.[36] The authors extended this notion, recommending that "other agencies would do well to heed the lessons of the federal government's chief accountability office as they go about the critical work of reinventing their own personnel systems.... In particular, GAO has five basic lessons to teach the rest of the federal government."[37] These are the need to move cautiously when pushing major change; the need for strong workforce planning; the need to emphasize more targeted recruitment, hiring, and retention policies; the need to beef up investments in systems for the selection and training of managers; and the need for a fair, unbiased, and transparent system for employee appeals.[38]

Despite this endorsement, the IBM study recognized that some executive agencies — the majority of whose personnel have moved out from under the traditional civil service — may be reluctant or limited in adopting the GAO model, in light of the important differences between GAO (a legislative branch support agency) and executive agencies that carry out public policy directly and immediately.[39] By comparison to GAO, these policy-implementing organizations are usually much larger; experience different levels of autonomy for entities within the agency or department; are more organizationally varied; and exhibit more functional diversity and mission multiplicity, resulting in cross-cutting and shared jurisdictions with other executive entities.

The GAO pay-for-performance implementation, along with similar efforts in executive agencies, have raised concerns over several matters in congressional hearings in the 110th Congress and other forums,[40] and have led to legislative proposals to modify the Comptroller General's powers in this regard (discussed above).[41] The issues include: whether the changes are implemented fairly and impartially across the board, whether the plan's criteria and standards are clear and appropriate, whether the measurements used to compare personnel in GAO and elsewhere lead to valid and reliable conclusions, whether the changes produce the desired results, whether they have an adverse effect on employee morale, and whether they prompt (or endorse) requests for similar authority in other government entities. Earlier, the office's pay-ban determinations had been challenged by 308 employees, resulting in a favorable settlement for 12.[42]

Employee Representation

As an outgrowth of the pay-for-performance dispute and other matters, eligible GAO analysts voted on September 19, 2007, to establish a local affiliate of the International Federation of Professional and Technical Employees (IFPTE), which will represent all bargaining unit employees on all matters that are subject to collective bargaining.[43] The new unit, supported by a two-to-one margin of the voting employees (among the 1,813 eligible), marks the first such employee organization in GAO history.[44]

Appointment of the Comptroller General and Deputy

Since its inception in 1921 as the General Accounting Office, the Government Accountability Office has been headed by only seven Comptrollers General.[45] **Table 2** lists them in chronological order.

When the Comptroller General post is vacant, GAO has been headed by an acting Comptroller General, as it is now. The longest absence of a confirmed Comptroller General was three years, 1936-1939. The second longest was the two-year vacancy from September 30, 1996, when Charles Bowsher ended his term, until November 9, 1998, when David Walker began his.

Current Process

Under GAO's current statutory charter, the Comptroller General and Deputy Comptroller General are nominated by the President, following recommendations from a special congressional commission, and are confirmed by the Senate.

When a vacancy occurs in the office of the Comptroller General or the Deputy, a special congressional commission, consisting of members of both chambers and both parties, is established to recommend individuals to the President for appointment.[46] Added by the General Accounting Office Act of 1980 (94 Stat. 314-315), this process became operational the following year. Under the arrangement, the recommending commission consists of the Speaker of the House, the President pro tempore of the Senate, the majority and minority leaders of the House and Senate, the chairmen and ranking minority members of the Senate Committee on Homeland Security and Governmental Affairs and the House Committee on Oversight and Government Reform, and, when the Deputy's post is vacant, the Comptroller General. The commission determines the criteria and standards for its nominees.

Table 2. Comptrollers General, 1921-Present

Comptroller General	Dates of Service
John Raymond McCarl	1921-1936
Fred Herbert Brown	1939-1940
Lindsay C. Warren	1940-1954
Joseph Campbell	1955-1965
Elmer B. Staats	1966-1981
Charles A. Bowsher	1981-1996
David M. Walker	1998-2008

The current process includes examination of the backgrounds and future plans of potential nominees, including, of course, their credentials, accomplishments, and relevant work experience in the private sector and public office. These examinations are conducted by the commission members and staff through interviews and meetings with the candidates, as well as with interested and knowledgeable parties, and a review of relevant materials and documents. Later examinations are held by the Senate Committee on Homeland Security and Governmental Affairs, which reports the nomination to the full Senate.[47]

The commission must recommend at least three individuals but the President may ask for additional names for consideration (or nominate someone else). The original bill called for five names to be submitted. However, the number was reduced, according to the report of the Senate Committee on Governmental Affairs, because "three names is a more realistic figure. Considering the high qualifications for the Office of Comptroller and Deputy Comptroller General, a requirement to generate five names might be extremely difficult to satisfy."[48]

The reporting panel also recognized that the President could still nominate an individual not recommended by the commission, in light of "the President's authority under the Appointments Clause .... However, it is expected that the President would give great weight to the Commission's recommendations."[49] This expectation has been met. On the two occasions since the 1980 enactment when a vacancy in the office of Comptroller General arose, Presidents Reagan in 1981 and Clinton in 1998 each selected a nominee from the initial congressional list.

The provision for a bicameral commission gives both chambers of Congress a formal and direct role in selecting the head of this legislative branch agency. The Senate Committee on Governmental Affairs endorsed the new arrangement:

> In view of the relationship between the Comptroller General and the Congress, the Committee believes it is appropriate that both Houses be given a role in the selection process.... [The new provision] reflects the special interests of both Houses in the choice of an individual whose primary function is to provide assistance to Congress.[50]

The current unique nomination process has not been used for the post of Deputy Comptroller General, which has remained vacant since the 1980 enactment. Instead of a confirmed Deputy, the Comptroller General has relied upon his own appointee(s) in one or two posts over the past several decades. Early in this period, a single special assistant to the Comptroller General served as second in command. Currently, two officials — the chief operating officer and the chief mission support officer — carry out the appropriate duties and functions.

Recent Nominations

The new nomination process went into effect in 1981, resulting in the appointment of Charles A. Bowsher, whose 15-year term expired in September, 1996.[51]

A second congressional commission met afterwards, to recommend a successor. On January 22, 1998, the commission sent the names of three individuals who "had received majority support from the members of the Commission" to President Clinton for his consideration, as provided in the 1980 statute.[52] Independently, six days later, Democratic members of the commission submitted four additional names.[53] On October 5, 1998, President Clinton nominated David M. Walker, one of the three original recommendations of the commission majority. He was confirmed by the Senate on October 21, following hearings by the Governmental Affairs Committee on October 7, and its favorable report on October 9.[54] Walker began his term of office on November 9, 1998.

The two-year interregnum marked the second longest period without a confirmed Comptroller General. And the nearly 10 months before the President submitted a nomination based on the congressional commission's recommendation prompted interest in making the Comptroller General position exclusively a legislative branch officer. But this was not acted on.[55] By so doing, Congress would have made the appointment itself, as it does, for instance, with the Director of the Congressional Budget Office.[56] (By comparison, other legislative branch offices —the Librarian of Congress, Architect of the Capitol, and Public Printer, who heads the Government Printing Office — are filled by presidential nominees who are confirmed by the Senate.)

Removal, Retirement, and Resignation

The Comptroller General is limited to a single 15-year term, a statutory provision[57] designed to protect the officer's independence, professional integrity, and objectivity. Of the seven Comptrollers General, three served the full term. (See **Table 2**.) The four with shorter tenures include David Walker, who will have served for nine years and four months when his resignation takes effect (November 9, 1998, to March 12, 2008). The remaining three who left early, coincidentally in succession, were Brown, one year, resignation; Warren, 14 years, retirement; and Campbell, 10½ years, retirement. All three cited ill health as the reason for leaving.

Removal

The Comptroller General or Deputy may be removed by impeachment or by adoption of a joint resolution of Congress. Removal by joint resolution can occur only after notice and an opportunity for a hearing and only for certain specified reasons: permanent disability, inefficiency, neglect of duty, malfeasance, felony conviction, or conduct involving moral turpitude. No Comptroller General or Deputy has been subject to either impeachment or removal by a joint resolution.

Retirement and Annuity

The current requirement creates an unequaled retirement system for the Comptroller General, by comparison with other government officials and employees. It provides that a CG who retires after at least 10 years in office "is entitled to receive an annuity for life equal to the pay the Comptroller General is receiving on completion of the term or at the time of retirement" (31 U.S.C. 772(a)).[58] In addition to this benefit, an annuity for a retired CG "shall be increased at the same time that, and by the same percent as the percentage by which, annuities are increased under section 8340(b) of Title 5" (31 U.S.C. 777(a)). As a qualification, this annuity "may not be more than the basic pay of the Comptroller General" (31 U.S.C. 777(b)).

This special retirement system was added in 1953.[59] In considering the legislation, the Senate Committee on Government Operations received the views of both the Civil Service Commission (CSC) and the Comptroller General. The Committee stated that the new retirement system for the Comptroller General was

> designed to conform to the particular nature of the office, which witnesses testified was similar in character, tenure and independence to the office of a Federal judge, and that its provisions are designed to conform to retirement benefits provided for Federal judges.[60]

The post was regarded as "unique," in a statement on behalf of the Chairman of the Civil Service Commission, who favored the retirement provision for several reasons.

> The Comptroller General is unique in that he is (a) independent of Executive control, (b) cannot be removed except by the Congress, and (c) is not eligible for reappointment after serving a 15-year term.[61]

A letter to the Committee from the CSC elaborated on these and other rationales. It noted that the Comptroller General's duties were "important and complex," demanding "the appointment of a mature man," who would not necessarily have had previous government experience and might not after leaving the post.[62] The resulting condition is that "upon completion of his term, the Comptroller General will normally be of such advanced age as to deter, if not prohibit, his acceptance of employment in other pursuits."[63]

Lindsay Warren, the Comptroller General at the time, echoed these sentiments. The fixed 15-year term, without the possibility of reappointment,

> is too long for such an officer to retain other ties, and too short to provide lifetime security or sufficient longevity to buy an annuity under the Civil Service Retirement System.... Important and complex duties of the position dictate the appointment of a mature man, who, upon completion of

> his term, would normally be beyond the age when he might seek new fields of activity.... the Office is a part of the legislative branch of the Government, and is of a semijudicial nature.[64]

An attempt to transform the CG's retirement system was advanced by the House Appropriations Committee in the 110th Congress. The panel included a proviso

> that repeals the unique Comptroller General Retirement system for any individual appointed Comptroller General after the enactment of this Act. Future appointments to this position will be covered under the standard Federal Employees Retirement System (FERS).[65]

Of the seven Comptrollers General, two — Lindsay Warren and Joseph Campbell — retired after going beyond the 10-year threshold (which was made available in 1954).[66]

Resignation

Throughout GAO's history, only two of the seven Comptrollers General have resigned from office. Fred Herbert Brown served a little over one year (April 11, 1939, to June 19, 1940), leaving office after suffering a stroke.[67] David M. Walker resigned in order to head a newly established public interest foundation.[68] He had served as Comptroller General for nine years and four months (November 9, 1998, to March 12, 2008), thus, falling short of the 10-year threshold to be eligible for the CG's retirement annuity.

Concluding Summary

Created in 1921, the General Accounting Office, now the Government Accountability Office, is Congress's largest support agency, with a budget of more than $507 million and an authorized staff of 3,100 for FY2008. The office has been headed by only seven comptrollers general over its eight-decade history; with a vacancy currently, it operates under an acting CG. GAO has been granted broad jurisdiction over the executive and substantial independence from it as well as extensive authority to gain access to its records and to investigate, audit, and evaluate its operations.[69] These attributes support a wide variety of services and activities, most connected with legislative oversight of the executive, that GAO can initiative on its own or, more usually, at the request of Congress, its Members, and panels.

Over the past decade, questions have arisen over several matters affecting GAO's structure, organization, and powers: the process (and resulting delay) for selecting the Comptroller General; the absence of a confirmed Deputy for more than twenty-five years; the unsuccessful attempt to gain access to information from a presidentially established panel, headed by the Vice President; problems in securing independent access to the records of certain agencies; and limitations on GAO auditing of all components of the intelligence community. As a result, bills have been introduced in the 110th Congress which would enhance GAO access to executive branch information, clarify the office's jurisdiction over the intelligence community, provide reimbursement for certain audit costs, and establish a statutory inspector general in GAO.

In the mid-1990s, GAO underwent a substantial downsizing — in funding and staffing — in part because of congressional criticism of its perceived orientation towards the previous two administrations and concerns about its missions and roles. In the meantime, the office has experienced a paradox between its budget and personnel levels. Its annual budget has increased regularly over the past 10 years —reaching its highest level in FY2008 — while its staff has been downsized, falling to its smallest level at the same time.

In 2004, the Comptroller General garnered new authority over pay and personnel in the newly-designated Government Accountability Office. A followup study a year later, under the auspices of the IBM Center for the Business of Government, found benefits in GAO's use of human capital management to drive its organizational transformation. The authors recommended that executive agencies —notwithstanding their differences with a legislative branch support agency — "heed the lessons of the government's chief accountability office as they go about the critical work of reinventing their own personnel systems." Despite this endorsement, the changes in GAO (as well as parallel ones in executive agencies) prompted concerns over the implementation and impact of the new personnel flexibilities authority and pay. These developments contributed, in 2007, to the establishment of an employee union with collective bargaining rights; in 2008, to a new contract for eligible employees; and in the same year, to legislative proposals to modify the CG's powers over such personnel matters and provide reimbursements for certain staff who did not receive pay increases in 2006 and 2007.

In sum, the Government Accountability Office appears to be going through a transition period. Changes — in progress or proposed — have been prompted by a vacancy in the office of the Comptroller General; the nearly 30-year absence of an official Deputy CG; conflicts over a new personnel system and its implementation; the perceived need for certain new arrangements and organizations within GAO, such as a statutory inspector general; and restrictions on its independent access to executive branch information and its auditing of the intelligence community.

End Notes

[1] The others are the Congressional Budget Office and the Congressional Research Service, along with other entities in the Library of Congress. A former support agency, the Office of Technology Assessment, was abolished in 1995; and the Government Printing Office serves different types of functions.

[2] U.S. Government Accountability Office, "David M. Walker, U.S. Comptroller General, Announces His Early Departure To Head New Public Interest Foundation," press release, February 15, 2008; Elizabeth Newell, "GAO chief announces resignation," *Government Executive*, available at [http://www.govexec.com/story_page.cfm?filepath=/dailyfed/0208/021508ts1.htm]; Elizabeth Williamson, "Government Accountability Chief Resigns," *Washington Post*, February 16, 2008, p. A7; Stephen Barr, "Comptroller General Leaving for Love of Country," *Washington Post*, March 10, 2008, pp. D1 and D4; Jordy Yager, "Comptroller General vacancy intensifies Bush-Hill battle," *The Hill*, available at [http://www.thehill.com], March 12, 2008; and Lindsey Layton, "Hunt for GAO Chief Is Complicated by Gridlock, Job's Unique Demands," *Washington Post*, Apr. 2, 2008, p. A17.

[3] Illustrations of products and services extend from identifying "high risk" areas in the executive, to conducting specialized investigations of criminal matters, to auditing a narrow project, to reviewing a broad program, to the Comptroller General making suggestions for congressional oversight topics. A summary of GAO's activities and services appears in CRS Report RL30240, *Congressional Oversight Manual*. For elaboration, see U.S. Senate Committee on Governmental Affairs, *Oversight of GAO: What Lies Ahead for Congress' Watchdog?* hearing, 108th Cong., 1st sess. (Washington: GPO, 2003); in addition to GAO publications, all of which are available from the Government Accountability Office: *Fiscal Stewardship: A Critical Challenge Facing Our Nation*, GAO-07-362SP (2007); *Fiscal Year 2008 Budget Request: U.S. Government Accountability Office*, GAO-07-547T (2007); *GAO: Transformation, Challenges, and Opportunities*, GAO-03-116T (2003); *GAO's Strategic Plan, 2007-2012*, GAO-07-1SP (2007); *Suggested Areas for Oversight for the 110th Congress*, letter to the Congressional Leadership, from Comptroller General David M. Walker, GAO-07-235R (2006); *U.S. General Accounting Office: The Role of GAO in Assisting Congressional Oversight*, statement by J. Christopher Mihm, GAO-02-816T (2002); and *United States Government Accountability Office: Supporting the Congress through Oversight, Insight, and Foresight*, statement of David M. Walker, Comptroller General, GAO-07-644T (2007).

[4] The office's criteria, standards, and procedures for responding to congressional requests are contained in U.S. General Accounting Office, *GAO's Congressional Protocols*, GAO-04-

310G (Washington: GAO, 2004). Its work with federal agencies is governed by *GAO's Agency Protocols*, GAO-03-232SP (Washington: GAO, 2002).

[5] For background on the establishment and evolution of GAO and the Comptroller General, see, among others: Darrell Hevenor Smith, *The General Accounting Office: Its History, Activities, and Organization* (Baltimore: Johns Hopkins University Press, 1927); Harvey C. Mansfield, *The Comptroller General* (New Haven, CT: Yale University Press, 1939); Thomas D. Morgan, "The General Accounting Office: One Hope for Congress to Regain Parity of Power with the President," *North Carolina Law Review*, vol. 51, October 1973, pp. 1279-1368; Frederick C. Mosher, *The GAO: The Quest for Accountability in American Government* (Boulder, CO: Westview Press, 1979); *A Tale of Two Agencies: A Comparative Analysis of the General Accounting Office and the Office of Management and Budget* (Baton Rouge, LA: Louisiana State University Press, 1984); Joseph Pois, *Watchdog on the Potomac: A Study of the Comptroller General of the United States* (Washington: University Press of America, 1979); Roger R. Trask, *GAO History, 1921-1991*, GAO Report OP-3-HP (Washington: GAO, 1991), along with a series of historical studies produced by GAO; U.S. Joint Committee on the Organization of Congress, *Support Agencies*, hearing, 103rd Cong., 1st sess. (Washington: GPO, 1993), pp. 5-27, 287-375; Frederick M. Kaiser, "The Comptroller General: History and Independence," in U.S. Senate Committee on Government Operations, Subcommittee on Reports, Accounting, and Management, *GAO Legislation*, hearing, 94th Cong., 1st sess. (Washington: GPO, 1975); U.S. Senate Committee on Governmental Affairs, *The Roles, Mission and Operation of the U.S. General Accounting Office: A Report by the National Academy of Public Administration*, Senate Print 103-87, 103rd Cong., 2nd sess. (Washington: GPO, 1994); Wallace E. Walker, *Changing Organizational Culture: Strategy, Structure, and Professionalism in the U.S. General Accounting Office* (Knoxville: University of Tennessee Press, 1986); and Jonathan Walters and Charles Thompson, *The Transformation of the Government Accountability Office: Using Human Capital to Drive Change* (Washington: IBM Center for The Business of Government, 2006).

[6] President Wilson's veto message and the House action, which sustained the veto by a vote of 178 to 103, are recorded in *Congressional Record*, vol. 59, June 4, 1920, pp. 8609-8613.

[7] Exceptions to GAO's jurisdiction over executive branch and independent agencies are (1) the Central Intelligence Agency, which views its own statutory authority as exempting it from GAO audits and reviews (e.g., the Central Intelligence Agency Act of 1949, 63 Stat. 213, and the General Accounting Office Act of 1980, 94 Stat. 311); and (2) foreign operations and money market policies of the Federal Reserve (31 U.S.C 714(b)). In addition, the President may proscribe GAO access to certain foreign intelligence and counterintelligence information and prevent its auditing of unvouchered funds involved in such areas (31 U.S.C. 716(b) and 3524(c)). This matter is discussed further below.

[8] For an overview of and further citations to GPRA and GAO's involvement, see U.S. General Accounting Office, *Executive Guide: Effectively Implementing the Government Performance and Results Act*, GAO Report GGD-96-118 (Washington: GAO, 1996); *Managing for Results: Using GPRA to Assist Congressional and Executive Branch Decisionmaking*, T-GGD-97-43 (Washington: GAO, 1997); and Mihm, *The Role of GAO in Assisting Congressional Oversight*.

[9] P.L. 106-312 established a three-year pilot program, whereby the Comptroller General would review any "economically significant rule" (e.g., a rule having an annual impact of $100 million on the economy or other specified economic effects), at the request of a chairman or ranking member of any committee of jurisdiction, and report his findings to Congress. Background information and debate on these proposals are included in: U.S. Congress, Senate Committee on Governmental Affairs, *Congressional Accountability for Regulatory Information Act of 1999; Report to Accompany S. 1198*, S.Rept. 106-225 (Washington: GPO, 1999); and *Congressional Record*, vol. 146, pp. S3782-S3785 and H6851-H6855.

[10] *Walker v. Cheney*, 230 F.Supp.2nd 51 (D.D.C., 2002). For further coverage, see Louis Fisher, "Congressional Access to Information: Using Legislative Will and Leverage," *Duke Law Journal*, vol. 52, 2002; CRS Report RL31397, *Walker v. Cheney: Statutory and Constitutional Issues Arising from the General Accounting Office's Suit Against the Vice President*, by T. J. Halstead; and T. J. Halstead, "*Walker v. Cheney*: Legal Insulation of the Vice President from GAO Investigations," *Presidential Studies Quarterly*, vol. 33, September 2003. The principals' statements are available at [http://oversight.house.gov/investigations.asp?ID=110]; Richard Cheney, U.S. Vice President, "Letter to the House of Representatives," August. 2, 2001; and U.S. General Accounting Office, "Statement on the NEPDG," 2001, "Letter to Vice President Cheney," July 18, 2001, "Report to the House of Representatives," August 17, 2001, and "Decision of the Comptroller General Concerning NEPDG Litigation," January 30, 2002, available at [http://www.gao.gov/cgdecnepdg.pdf].

[11] Government Accountability Act of 2008, H.R. 6388, 110th Cong., 2nd sess. U.S. Congress, House Committee on Oversight and Government Reform, "Statement of Rep. Henry A. Waxman on the Introduction of the Government Accountability Act," June 26, 2008; "Committee Chairs Introduce Bill to Strengthen GAO," Press release, June 27, 2008; and *Government Accountability Act of 2008*, H.Rept. 110-771, 110th Cong., 2nd sess. See also, Dan Friedman, "Panel approves bill allowing GAO to sue agencies," *Government Executive*, July 16, 2008, available at [http://www.govexec.com/story_page.cfm?articleid=40484&dcn=e_gvet]; Ralph Lindeman, "House Approves Measure to Give GAO Additional Investigative Powers," *Daily Report for Executives*, BNA, Inc., July 30, 2008, p. A-1; and "House bill would give GAO more clout," *Federal Times*, Aug. 4, 2008, p. 4.

[12] David M. Walker, *Commercial Activities Panel: Improving Sourcing Decisions of the Federal Government*, GAO-02-866T, June 26, 2002; and U.S. Commercial Activities Panel, *Improving Sourcing Decisions of the Government: Final Report* (Washington: CAP, 2002).

[13] Sec. 251, P.L. 99-177, 99 Stat. 1038 (1985).

[14] *Bowsher v. Synar*, 478 U.S. 714, at 734 (1986).

[15] U.S. Congress, House Committee on Oversight and Government Reform, Subcommittee on Federal Workforce, Postal Service, and the District of Columbia, *GAO Personnel Reform*, hearings, 110th Cong., 1st sess., May 22, 2007; *Government Accountability Act of 2007*, hearings, 110th Cong., 2nd sess., March 13, 2008, and *Government Accountability Office Act of 2008: Report to Accompany H.R. 5683*, H.Rept. 110-671, 110th Cong., 2nd sess., both available at [http://federalworkforce.oversight.house.gov/story.asp?ID=1804]; and "Government Accountability Act of 2008," *Congressional Record*, daily ed., June 9, 2008, vol. 154, pp. H5080-H5084, and *Congressional Record*, daily ed., Aug. 1, 2008, vol 154, pp S8070-S8073. See also Dan Friedman, "Panel targets GAO pay system," March 13, 2008, and "Houses passes GAO pay bill, minus investigative provisions," June 10, 2008, and Brittany R. Ballenstedt, "Lawmakers seek remedy for GAO pay reform," March 14, 2008, "Panel approves bill to restore back raises to GAO employees," May 23, 2008; "Senate passes bill to restore back pay to GAO employees," Aug. 4, 2008; and "House sends GAO pay bill to President Bush," Sept. 9, 2008; all in *Government Executive*, available at [http://www.govexec.com/story_page_pf.cfm?articleid]; and Nancy Ognanovich, "After Senate Vote, Conference Likely on Legislation to Reform, Strengthen GAO," *Daily Report for Executives*, BNA, Inc., Aug. 5, 2008, p. A-7.

[16] 5 U.S.C. Appendix. For background, see CRS Report 98-379, *Statutory Offices of Inspector General: Past and Present*, by Frederick M. Kaiser.

[17] Citations in note 10 above.

[18] Citations in note 11 above.

[19] See note 7 for statutory citations.

[20] Background to the conflict is covered in Frederick M. Kaiser, "GAO Versus the CIA: Uphill Battles Against an Overpowering Force," *International Journal of Intelligence and Counterintelligence*, vol. 15, Summer 2003, pp. 330-389.

[21] The Intelligence Community Audit Act, H.R. 978 and S. 82, 110th Cong. U.S. Congress, Senate Subcommittee on Oversight of Government Management, the Federal Workforce, and the District of Columbia, *Government-wide Intelligence Community Management Reforms*, hearings, 110th Cong., 2nd sess., Feb. 29, 2008, available at [http://hsgac.senate.gov/ index.cfm?Fuseaction=Hearings.Detail&HearingID=526].

[22] Department of Defense Instruction 7650.02, November 20, 2006.

[23] Elaboration of GAO's support for such new authority and the DNI's (and the previous DCI's) opposition appears in: letter from David M. Walker, Comptroller General, to Hon. John D. Rockefeller, Chairman, and Hon. Christopher S. Bond, Vice Chairman, Senate Select Committee on Intelligence, March 1, 2007; and letter from J. M. McConnell, Director of National Intelligence, to Hon. John D. Rockefeller, Chairman, and Christopher S. Bond, Vice Chairman, Senate Select Committee on Intelligence, Mar. 7, 2007. See M.Z. Hemingway, "GAO wants more muscle," *Federal Times*, March 26, 2007, p. 1; and "GAO Seeks Greater Role in Oversight of Intelligence," *Secrecy News*, Oct. 3, 2007, available at [http://www.fas.org]. For the competing views of the disputes over independent GAO access, which date to the earliest days of the CIA, see U.S. Central Intelligence Agency, *DCI Affirmation of Policy for Dealing with the General Accounting Office (GAO)*, Memorandum for the Director of Central Intelligence, from Stanley L. Moskowitz, Director of Congressional Affairs, 7 July 1994; U.S. General Accounting Office, *Central Intelligence Agency: Observations on GAO Access to Information on CIA Programs and Activities*, statement of Henry J. Hinton, GAO-01-975T (2001); letters from the Comptroller General to the Director of National Intelligence (DNI), April 27, 2006, and to the Chairman and Ranking Minority Member of the Senate Committee on Homeland Security and Governmental Affairs, May 15, 2006, disagreeing with the DNI's position that the "review of intelligence activities is beyond the GAO's purview," as stated in *Information Sharing*, GAO-06-385 (2006), pp. 6 and 71.

[24] H.R. 978 and S. 82, 110th Congress. See U.S. Congress, Senate Subcommittee on Oversight of Government Management, the Federal Workforce, and the District of Columbia, *Government-wide Intelligence Community Reform*, hearings, 110th Cong., 2nd sess., February 29, 2009, available at [http://hsgac.senate.gov/indx.cfm?Fuseaction= Hearings]; and "Panel witnesses press for GAO audits of intelligence agencies," *Government Executive*, available at [http://www.govexec.com/story_page.cfm?filepath=/ dailyfed/0208/022908cdpm2.htm], February 29, 2008.

[25] Legislative Reorganization Act of 1994, S. 1824, 103rd Congress. The House and Senate Members of the Joint Committee issued separate reports, but both agreed to the specific recommendation of ending the permanent authorization status for congressional support agencies. U.S. Congress, Joint Committee on the Organization of the Congress, *Organization of the Congress: Final Report of the House Members*, H.Rept. 103-413, vol. I, 103rd Cong., 1st sess., p. 20, and *Organization of the Congress: Final Report of the Senate Members*, S.Rept. 103-215, 103rd Cong., 1st sess. (Washington: GPO, 1993), p. 17.

[26] James F. Hinchman, Acting Comptroller General, U.S. General Accounting Office, *Fiscal Year 1998 Budget Estimates for the U.S. General Accounting Office*, GAO T-OCG-97-01 (Washington: GAO, 1997), p. 4. See also *GAO's Downsizing Efforts*, GAO T-OCG-96-4 (Washington: GAO, 1996).

[27] U.S. Congress, House Subcommittee on Legislative Appropriations, *Legislative Branch Appropriations for 2000*, hearings, 106th Cong., 1st sess. (Washington: GPO, 1999), part 2, pp. 203-204. Also, see GAO testimonies on this matter: T-OCG-99-22 and T-OCG-99-24 (Washington: GAO, 1999), pp. 8-10 and 19.

[28] In fact, GAO's FY2009 budget submission asserted that "(o)ur FTE level in fiscal year 2008 is 3,100 — the lowest level ever for GAO." GAO, *Fiscal Year 2009 Budget Request*, GAO-08-616, p. 4.

[29] U.S. Senate Committee on Governmental Affairs, *General Accounting Office Personnel Act of 1979*, S.Rept. 96-540, 96th Cong., 1st sess. (Washington: GPO, 1979), p. 2.

[30] Ibid.

[31] An article on changes at GAO at the time is by Susannah Zak Figura, "The Human Touch," *Government Executive*, September 2000, pp. 22-27.

[32] See U.S. Congress, Senate Committee on Governmental Affairs, *GAO Human Capital Reform Act of 2003*, S.Rept. 108-216, 108th Cong., 1st sess. (Washington: GPO, 2003); U.S. Congress, House Committee on Government Reform, *GAO Human Capital Reform Act of 2003*, H.Rept. 108-380 (Washington: GPO, 2003); U.S. Congress, House Committee on Government Reform and Senate Committee on Governmental Affairs, hearings on H.R. 2751 and S. 1522, 108th Cong., 1st sess., respectively; U.S. General Accounting Office, *GAO: Additional Human Capital Flexibilities Are Needed*, Statement by David M. Walker, Comptroller General, Report GAO-03-1024T (Washington: GAO, 2003); and U.S. General Accounting Office, *GAO's Proposed Human Capital Legislation: View of the Employee Advisory Council*, Statement by Christopher A. Keisling, Council Member, Report GAO-03-1020T (Washington: GAO, 2003); and GAO, *Fiscal Year 2004 Budget Request (2003)*. A summary of GAO's implementation appears in GAO, *2006 Report on GAO's Use of the Provisions in the GAO Personnel Flexibilities Act of 2000 and the GAO Human Capital Reform Act of 2004*, Report GAO-07-289SP (2007). See also Mollie Ziegler, "GAO shifts to market wages," *Federal Times*, January 28, 2005, p. 1; and Stephen Barr, "GAO Chief Aims to Raise the Bar on Pay Raises," *Washington Post*, July 6, 2003, p. C2, and "Other Agencies May Learn from GAO's Pay, Classification Review," *Washington Post*, May 13, 2004, p. B2.

[33] GAO contracted with Watson Wyatt to assist in developing a new market-based compensation system for the agency's employees. "Contract Awarded to Develop Market-Based Pay Scales for Analysts, Attorneys, and Specialists," *GAO Management News*, vol. 31, July 26-30, 2004.

[34] Walker, *GAO: Additional Human Capital Flexibilities Are Needed*, p. 5. For elaboration, see also David M. Walker, "GAO: A Case Study in Human Capital Reform," *The Federal Manager*, Spring 2008, pp. 3-7; and GAO, *U.S. Government Accountability Office: Human Capital Initiatives and Additional Legislative Authorities,* GAO-08-573T, statement of Gene L. Dodaro, Acting Comptroller General of the United States (Washington: GAO, 2008).

[35] Walters and Thompson, *The Transformation of GAO*.

[36] Ibid., p. 4. In terms of its review of GAO's experience, however, the IBM report has certain limitations. Importantly, it does not provide details about the methodology used to analyze and assess the office's new personnel system, the changes it generated, and their perceived impact, raising some questions about its reliability. The study, for instance, neglects to spell out the interview schedule, questions asked, and characteristics of the participants (e.g., upper versus lower grade levels, organization officials versus employee association leaders, and management versus staff). The review also reports data from a GAO employee feedback survey supporting its findings about perceived improvements in the organizational climate, staff development, staff utilization, and leadership. The survey lists the percent of employees responding favorably to particular statements, including differences between staff and upper level management. Ibid., pp. 25-26. But the perceived improvements from 2003 to 2004 increase from only 1% to 3% for the average in each category. Perhaps because the levels were in the 60 and 70 percentage range, the increases do not appear to be statistically significant. Furthermore, the report neither discusses how the survey was developed and administered nor provides data on several workforce characteristics which could put the responses into a comparative perspective: missing, for example, are the number of respondents (in totality and in each area) as well as their representativeness of the GAO workforce in terms of staff, management positions, grade level, and seniority as well as gender and race.

[37] Ibid., p. 6.

[38] Ibid. Other organizational transformations — based on the "best practices" from the public and private sector, regarding open communications between employees and management, centralized authority and accountability, and senior management open support for new policies and programs — are also contained in the report. Ibid., pp. 20 and 24.

[39] Ibid., pp. 5-6 and 22. The inability or piecemeal approach to a similar transformation could arise because of differences between a policy-implementing executive agency and a legislative support agency (in terms of missions, functions, authority, organization, and procedures). It could also arise because of concerns from some stakeholders, such as federal employee unions, about several matters: whether certain executive agencies could meet the GAO standards (due to different organizational cultures and conditions, for instance); what unintended consequences might occur; how the new managerial powers might be manipulated or misused; and what the full cost of implementation would be.

[40] See citations in notes 15 and 32, above, along with U.S. House Subcommittee on the Federal Workforce, Postal Service, and District of Columbia, *Status of Federal Personnel Reform*, hearing, 110th Cong., 1st sess., March 8, 2007, and *Government Accountability Act of 2007*, hearing, 110th Cong., 2nd sess., March 13, 2008; and jointly with the Senate Subcommittee on Government Management, the Federal Workforce, and the District of Columbia, *GAO's Personnel Reform Efforts,* joint hearing, 110th Cong., 1st sess., May 22, 2007. Press coverage appears in: Brittany R. Ballenstedt, "Lawmakers probe GAO decision on pay adjustments," March 7, 2007, "Lawmakers grill GAO chief over pay decisions," May 22, 2007, "GAO to challenge eligibility of employees to unionize," June 1, 2007, "Lawmakers seek remedy for GAO pay reform," March 14, 2008, and "GAO to seek input from employees on changes to new pay system," April 10, 2008, all in *Government Executive*, available at [http://www.govexec.com]; Dan Friedman, "Panel targets GAO pay system," *Government Executive*, March 13, 2008, available at [http://www.govexec.com]; Kelly McCormack, "Subcommittee hears testimony on GAO pay system," *The Hill*, March 13, 2007, p. 6; M. Z. Hemingway, "Comptroller general pans CRS study of GAO pay," *Federal Times*, March 12, 2007, p. 1; and Stephen Barr, "Congress Questions Pay Restructuring at GAO," *Washington Post*, May 23, 2007, p. D4.

[41] H.R. 5683, which passed the House, and S. 2564, 110th Cong., 2nd sess. See also citations in note 15 above.

[42] In early 2007, 12 of the 308 employees reached a settlement with GAO, receiving compensation benefits as if they had been promoted a year before. The employees had filed an appeal before the GAO Appeals Board (U.S. Government Accountability Office, Personnel Appeals Board, *Petitioner v. Government Accountability Office, Respondent*, February 2006). The settlement was reached, however, before a hearing was held; and the claims were not adjudicated by the Board. Press coverage by Britanny R. Ballenstedt, "GAO settles pay dispute with 12 of 308 senior analysis," April 27, 2007, *Government Executive* at [http://www.govexec.com].

[43] "CG Discusses Immediate Impact of Union Election on GAO Operations," *GAO Management News*, vol. 35, October 15, 2007, p. 1; and *Joint Statement of the Government Accountability Office and the International Federation of Professional and Technical Engineers*, July 18, 2007. For background and press coverage, see U.S. House Committee on Appropriations, *Legislative Branch Appropriations Bill, 2008*, H.Rept. 110-198, 110th Cong., 1st sess., p. 33; Britanny R. Ballenstedt, "Union to file for first-ever election at GAO," May 7, 2007, "More than 200 GAO employees to petition for back pay," May 15, 2007, "GAO to challenge eligibility of employees to unionize," June 1, 2007, "Union files unfair labor practice charge against GAO chief," June 22, 2007, "GAO, union reach agreement to hold election," July 19, 2007, "GAO analysts vote for union representation," Sept. 20, 2007, and "Rising Expectations," November 7, 2007; Karen Rutzick, "GAO employees move toward vote on union representation," January 23, 2007, all in *Government Executive* [http://www.govexec.com]; M.Z. Hemingway, "Labor strife hits GAO," *Federal Times*, May 14, 2007, p. 4, and "GAO chief fights to keep union out," *Federal Times*, June

11, 2007, p. 1; Richard W. Walker, "GAO analysts vote for union representation," at [http://www.FCW.com]; and Stephen Barr, "In a First, GAO Analysts Vote to Join a Union," *Washington Post*, September 21, 2007, p. D4.

44 In early 2008, the union and GAO reached a tentative contract agreement, which affects employee pay scales, including those based on performance ratings, as well as eligibility for annual pay increases. Brittany Ballenstedt, "GAO, union reach agreement on 2008 pay raises," *Government Executive,* available at [http://www.govexec.com/story_page.cfm?filepath=/dailyfed/0208/021108b1.htm], February 11, 2008; and Stephen Barr, "GAO and Its New Union Reach Agreement on Raises, *Washington Post*, February 12, 2008, p. D4.

45 See note 2, above; and Trask, *GAO History*, pp. 7-20, 22, 25-38, 43-57, and 59-94.

46 A proposal from GAO would change the process for the deputy, by allowing the CG to appoint the deputy, after consultation with the congressional commission (H.R. 3268, 110th Congress, described above).

47 For the most recent illustration, see U.S. Congress, Senate Committee on Governmental Affairs, *Nominations of Edward J. Gleiman, Dana B. Covington, and David M. Walker*, hearings, 105th Cong., 2nd sess. (Washington: GPO, 1998), pp. 17-18 and 70-130.

48 U.S. Congress, Senate Committee on Governmental Affairs, *General Accounting Office Act of 1980*, S.Rept. 96-570, 96th Cong., 2nd sess. (Washington: GPO, 1980), p. 10. Despite the scaling back to three recommendations, eight names were submitted the first time the new procedure was used, in 1981.

49 Ibid.

50 Ibid., p. 9.

51 U.S. Congress, Senate Committee on Governmental Affairs, *Nomination of Charles A. Bowsher*, hearing, 97th Cong., 1st sess. (Washington: GPO, 1981); "Nomination of Charles A. Bowsher to Be Comptroller General of the United States," *Congressional Record*, vol. 127, September 29, 1981; and U.S. President Ronald Reagan, "Remarks Announcing Intention to Nominate Charles A. Bowsher" (July 9, 1981), *Public Papers of the Presidents: Ronald Reagan, 1981* (Washington: GPO, 1982), pp. 612-614. Bowsher was one of eight persons recommended by the commission, which had an equal number of Democrats and Republicans. See Trask, *GAO History*, p. 97; "Accountant Bowsher Named New GAO Head," *Congressional Quarterly*, July 18, 1981, p. 1301; and Greg Rushford, "Veteran of Capital Hardball Chosen for Top GAO Post," *Federal Times*, July 20, 1981, p. 6.

52 Letter from Senate Majority Leader Trent Lott and Speaker of the House Newt Gingrich, to President William Clinton, January 22, 1998, regarding recommendations for Comptroller General. See also Stephen Barr, "GOP Leaders Offer Three to Head GAO," *Washington Post*, January 27, 1998, p. A15.

53 "Democrats, Objecting to Republican Move, Send 7 Names to Clinton for GAO," *Washington Post*, February 2, 1998, p. A17.

54 *Congressional Record*, vol. 144, October 21, 1998, p. S12980. See also Robert Pear, "A C.P.A. at Center Stage: David Michael Walker," *New York Times*, October 23, 1998, p. A14; and Senate Committee on Governmental Affairs, *Nomination of... David M. Walker*.

55 "GOP May Seek to Strip Clinton of Power to Name GAO Head," *CQ Daily Monitor*, July 29, 1998, p. 5.

56 Earlier proposals along this line, incidentally, were raised in the mid-1970s, prior to the change setting up the congressional commission to make recommendations to the President. See Mosher, *The GAO*, p. 288. The bills introduced in 1975 were H.R. 8616, 94th Cong., 1st sess., sponsored by Rep. Jack Brooks, and S. 2066, 94th Cong., 1st sess., sponsored by Sen. Lee Metcalf, with hearings on the latter. U.S. Congress, Senate Committee on Government Operations, Subcommittee on Reports, Accounting, and Management, *GAO Legislation*, hearing, part 1, 94th Cong., 1st sess. (Washington: GPO, 1975).

57 31 U.S.C. 43.

58 A Comptroller General separated from office before becoming entitled to receive an annuity under this section is "entitled to lump-sum refund of the amount deducted from pay or

deposited as a contribution under section 772, plus 3 percent interest on the amount compounded every December 31" (31 U.S.C. 775(a). A Comptroller General has another option available with regard to a retirement program, if he or she is already a federal employee. A CG who, when appointed, is under the Civil Service Retirement System (CSRS) or the Federal Employee Retirement System (FERS) remains subject to it, unless the Comptroller General elects in writing to receive the special life-time annuity. Such an election is irrevocable and must be made within 10 years and 60 days after the start of service as Comptroller General. A CG electing the special life-time annuity instead of remaining under CSRS or FERS is entitled to a refund of the lump-sum credit to the account of the Comptroller General in the Civil Service Retirement and Disability Fund. (31 U.S.C. 772(c).

[59] P.L. 83-161, Comptroller General — Retirement.

[60] U.S. Congress, Senate Committee on Government Operations, *Comptroller General, Retirement*, S.Rept. 594, 83rd Cong., 1st sess. (Washington: GPO, 1953), p. 1.

[61] Ibid., pp. 1-2.

[62] Letter from the Acting Assistant Executive Director, Civil Service Commission, July 15, 1953, to Hon. Joseph R. McCarthy, Chairman, Senate Committee on Government Operations. Ibid. pp. 3-4

[63] Ibid., p. 4.

[64] Letter from Lindsay Warren, Comptroller General, ibid.

[65] U.S. House Committee on Appropriations, *Legislative Branch Appropriations Act, 2008*, H.Rept. 110-198, 110th Cong., 1st sess., p. 34. The proposal was eliminated in conference.

[66] Trask, *History of GAO*, pp. 38 and 57.

[67] Ibid., p. 22.

[68] See note 2 above.

[69] GAO is one of a number of comparable organizations worldwide — collectively known as Supreme Audit Institutions (SAIs) — that audit, investigate, and/or review government activities, operations, and programs. These counterparts have similar but not identical responsibilities, functions, powers, and degrees of independence (from the entities they audit and investigate), reflected to a degree in their different titles: e.g., the Supreme Chamber of Control (Poland), Court of Audit (Belgium), Office of the Comptroller and Auditor General (Ireland), National Audit Office and Northern Ireland Audit Office (United Kingdom), Tribunal of Contras (Portugal), and Cour des Comptes (France). Descriptions of these and other similar offices are found in: International Organization of Supreme Audit Institutions, *Survey and Description of Selective National Audit Offices* (loose-leaf collection) (Vienna: INTOSAI, 1996); National Audit Office, *State Audit in the European Union* (London: NAO, 1996); S. N. Swaroop, *Supreme Audit Institutions in Different Countries* (New Delhi: Ashish Publishing House, 1991). Although there is no current, broad-scale, systematic comparison of SAIs internationally, GAO probably ranks highest across such key criteria as independence, authority, jurisdiction, functions, and resources. Along these lines, a comparison between GAO and its UK counterpart concluded that "the powers, duties, and self-perception of the National Audit Office [UK] are significantly weaker and more mutable than those of the Government Accountability Office." Simon D. Norton and L. Murphy Smith, "Contrast and Foundation of the Public Oversight Roles of the U.S. Government Accountability Office and the U.K. National Audit Office," *Public Administration Review*, Sept./Oct. 2008, p. 921.

INDEX

H

I

J

L

M

N

O

P

Q

R

S